William M'Dowall

Among the Old Scotch Minstrels

Studying their Ballads of War, Love, Social Life, Folk-lore and Fairyland

William M'Dowall

Among the Old Scotch Minstrels

Studying their Ballads of War, Love, Social Life, Folk-lore and Fairyland

ISBN/EAN: 9783744776936

Printed in Europe, USA, Canada, Australia, Japan

Cover: Foto ©Thomas Meinert / pixelio.de

More available books at **www.hansebooks.com**

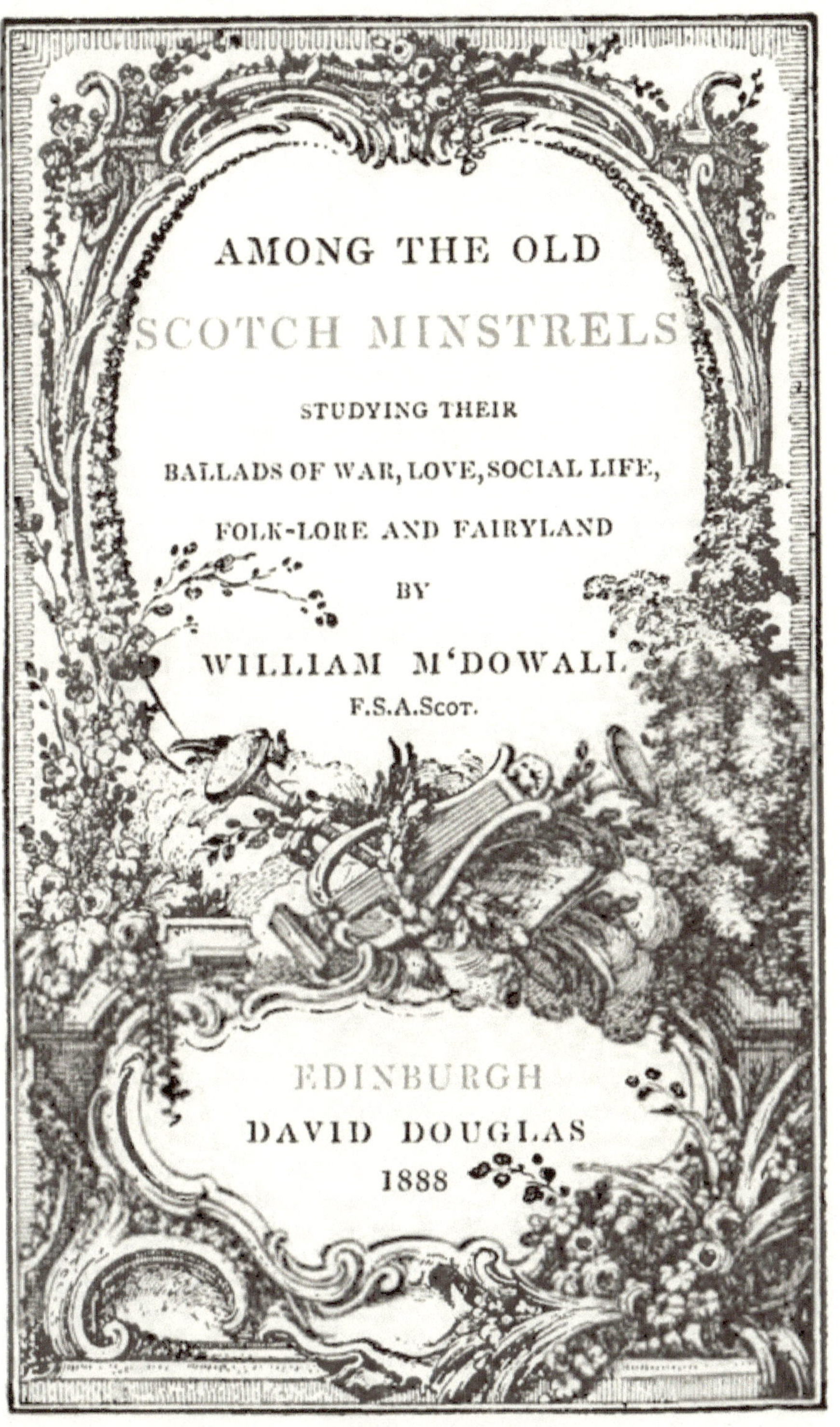
AMONG THE OLD
SCOTCH MINSTRELS
STUDYING THEIR
BALLADS OF WAR, LOVE, SOCIAL LIFE,
FOLK-LORE AND FAIRYLAND
BY
WILLIAM M'DOWALL
F.S.A.Scot.
EDINBURGH
DAVID DOUGLAS
1888

PREFACE

NOT a few students of the Old Scottish Ballads have endeavoured, with less or more success, to identify their heroes and heroines with real personages, to fix with some degree of precision the scenery of the incidents, and to ascertain the historical value of such metrical tales as relate to matters of national importance. Into these well-traversed fields of inquiry the author of this volume has rarely ventured. He has approached the ballads in a sympathetic spirit, accepting them as the genuine utterances of men who made it their business and their pleasure to instruct and entertain the public, and had full faith in their mission. He has aimed at being descriptive rather than critical; as the ballads are the product of a credulous age, and were addressed to believing audiences, he has listened to them with

a receptive ear.   When entering the circle of
the old minstrels, it was with uncovered head
and reverential step, and to become, as it
were, a humble but loving disciple, luxuriat-
ing in the romantic atmosphere which they
breathe, the unconventional sentiment—
delicate yet bold, ' tender and true '—which
they express, in verse that is rarely common-
place, and is often richly musical.

Fully sixty ballads are studied in the
text, these comprising nearly all the best
productions of their kind now extant.   The
author is aware that certain able critics
have looked upon some of them as mere
imitations ; but he is of opinion that all
the pieces he has dealt with carry as cre-
dentials the unmistakable hoar and flavour
of antiquity.   It will be seen that he has
adopted a new classification, the divisions
being into historical and warlike, border and
warlike, tragical, amatory and tragical, melo-
dramatic, and mythological, which may
perhaps meet with the reader's approval,
even though several of the ballads given
in one group possess features in common

with those of other sections. The author may perhaps be permitted to add that some ten of the 'studies' are thirty years old. that the others were produced within the last fourteen months, and that the more he mixes with the old Scottish minstrels the better he likes their company.

17 CRESSWELL TERRACE,
  DUMFRIES, *5th June*, 1888.

CONTENTS

AMONG THE OLD SCOTCH MINSTRELS.

FROM a remote period down till the present day Scotland has continued to produce a race of famous poets, so that the air of the country has become vocal with strains that are racy of the soil. More recently Ramsay, Fergusson, Burns, Scott, Hogg, Tannahill, Campbell, Cunningham, and a host of other bards, have embalmed their names in imperishable verse, and full justice has been done by fame to the claims of these masters of the lyre, some of them the mightiest that ever struck its strings. But the minstrels of the olden time—the grey fathers of Scottish song—the ballad-makers and harpers who in the dim twilight of the historic era charmed the ear of kings and peasants, and launching their lyrical creations on the stream of tradition, left them as a legacy to future ages—of these men, to whom we are so much indebted, nothing is personally known—even their names have perished, and we are unable to inscribe them on the roll of fame, and pay meet homage to their individual worth.   Literally it may be said of them, they are a voice and nothing more—a rich voice singing in the wilderness of the middle ages; or we might apply to each of these ancient poets what Shelley says of the unseen skylark scattering unpremeditated notes of wild delight from its high aërial tower :—

> All the earth and air
>   With thy voice is loud,
> As, when night is bare,
>   From one lonely cloud
> The moon rains out her beams and heaven is
>   overflowed.

> What thou art we know not ;
>   What is most like thee ?
> From rainbow clouds there flow not
>   Drops so bright to see
> As from thy presence showers a rain of melody.

The effusions of the old balladists might have perished with them—and probably that would have been their fate, had they been tame, artificial, and commonplace; but possessing as they do natural truthfulness, genuine simplicity, and a rare mixture of rough vigour with touches of inimitable tenderness, and appealing as they do to the strongest emotions of our common humanity, they took hold of the memory of their hearers, who treasured them there, and transmitted them to other delighted listeners. And thus, though very few of the ballads were written, and still fewer printed, till the beginning of the eighteenth century, they were carefully handed down from mother to daughter, from sire to son; and they are now—let us be thankful for it—in the custody of printed books, where they will remain safe and also popular, so long as the language endures—or, I might say, so long as pure, artless poetry exercises a commanding influence over the human heart.

There was great danger of many of these relics of bygone times being irrecoverably lost when the printer's art got into general use. It was so much easier to read a tale or poem than commit it to memory, that the latter practice fell into disuse, and was in a great measure confined to old people; and it was they who about one hundred and eighty years ago held in the casket of their memories nearly all these gems of minstrelsy; and it would in all probability have been buried in

their graves, had not such men as Percy, Herd,
Pinkerton, Ritson, Motherwell, Sharpe, and
Scott stepped in at this critical transition
period, and secured the precious waifs, which
would soon have been lost for ever.

Though the personality of the old minstrels
has been lost in the mist of ages, yet we know
something about them as a class, and, guided
by Scott, Tytler, Professor Aytoun, and other
writers on the subject, I shall endeavour to
present the reader with an idea of their pro-
fessional character and position, first glancing,
however, at the principal features of the period
in which they flourished.

Some specimens of our ballad poetry are
extant which date as far back as the middle
of the fourteenth century; and there can be no
doubt that at a much earlier period the lyrical
muse of Scotland was invoked with success.
John Barbour, born in 1316, celebrated the
achievements of Bruce in verse of appropriate
nerve and vigour, and may be looked upon as
the father of the northern minstrels. From
his day down till about the close of the
seventeenth century is the grand ballad epoch
of which, and its products, I mean to treat.
During that period of three hundred and fifty
years a considerable change took place in the
character of the inhabitants; but for the
greater part of it they were comparatively

rude — war the principal occupation of all ranks, the chase their chief out-of-door pastime, while their brief in-door leisure was wiled away by feast and song, the brimming wassail bowl, and the minstrel's harp. In such circumstances what themes could the poet choose as most likely to be popular but those which signalised the active current of existence? He became, as it were, the reproducer and echo of the doughty achievements in which his patrons took delight, and which filled the public mind, and, accordingly, the excitement and perils of the boar-hunt and the deer-chase, the strife of feudal barons, adventurous raids across the Border, and the national battles of the kingdoms into which Britain was divided, figure largely in the minstrel's verse; and, inasmuch as even in that wild age "Love ruled the court, the camp, the grove," the influence of the tender passion for weal or woe, its happy progress— or, more frequently, its rugged course and tragic issues, received due prominence in the minstrel's ditties. Then, the age was extremely superstitious — a belief in the existence of fairies, in the frequent appearance of wraiths, ghosts, and water-kelpies, in the power of old women to make compacts with the Prince of Darkness, and thereby to perform marvellous feats of malignity—a belief of all this was universal, and, as a matter of course, it tinctured the ballad-poetry of the times.

Many of the ballads are pervaded by an eerie, unearthly sort of influence, while others are entirely devoted to the fantastic pranks of mischievous elves, or the doings of strange human folks—half material, half spiritual—who are sometimes represented as rising from the graveyard ; and at other times as coming from the land unseen to haunt an enemy, to revenge a wrong, or claim back troth from the lips of a perjured lover. In all these respects the ballad minstrelsy of Scotland is a record and a reflex of the manners and creeds of the time when it was composed and sung, and hence it has no small historic value, apart altogether from its poetic merits.

Many instances of ferocity, many deeds of dreadful note, and not a few examples of unbridled lust, form the burden of the old ballads ; and in no respect are they more truthful transcripts of the age when they were produced. But the same verse which tells us of desperate crime gives us fine glimpses of domestic affection, of self-denying true love, of patient endurance, of heroic magnanimity, of unswerving truth, and incorruptible patriotism, proving that if crime abounded, the public and personal virtues were not overborne by it, even in the mid-

night of the period when the maxim was habi-
tually acted upon—

" That they should take who have the power,
    And they should keep who can."

" Tragic enough, certainly," says a writer in
Blackwood's Magazine, " are the plot and inci-
dents of the Scottish ballads, desperately
wicked sometimes the perpetrators, male or
female. But still through the histories of their
misdeeds, the narrative conveys in some shape
—whether that of an avenging Providence or
the milder medium of some great man's judg-
ment—a commendation of honour, truth, fidel-
ity, and all those virtues which are the best
that men can exercise towards each other."
Some writers on the subject suppose that
to a large extent the ballads were produced as
" voices from the crowd " by poets who sprang
up promiscuously among the common people ;
others consider that we owe them chiefly to
professional bards who served in the house-
holds of our kings and great nobles, and to
other trained minstrels who depended princi-
pally on the general public for patronage—
the latter travelling from hut to hall reciting
or singing the products of their fancy, and re-
ceiving in return board, bed, and largess from
those who listened to their lyrics. That there
did exist for several hundred years before the

Union a craft or body of men, some of whom at least sang their own compositions, and whose calling was as distinct as that of the priest or warrior, is unquestionable, though the likelihood I think is, that many of the effusions to which they gave the music of harp and voice were written by men who bore the shepherd's crook, the herdsman's staff, or the brand of battle, or even, in later days, by douce denizens of burgh towns engaged in the prosaic vocation of fabricating or vending the rude wares of the period. We know that in the reign of James V. a taste for poetry pervaded all ranks, and we may be sure that it would give rise to many spontaneous productions — the very breath of popular feeling, and that thereby the repertoire of the wandering minstrel would be greatly enriched. Any one conversant with the ballads must have observed that stereotyped lines, and even verses, occur that are common to many of them. just as there are some newspaper phrases in general use among the brethren of the broadsheet. When these are found in any ballad, I set it down as having been written, or, at all events, adapted by a professional minstrel; and the ballads in which they are wanting, and which possess in other respects a superior amount of individuality, I am inclined to assign to anonymous amateurs who felt they had something to say, and found a pleasure in wedding their thoughts to verse, while they were further rewarded by the knowledge that, if worthy to live, they would be scattered wide over the land by voice and lyre.

We may safely conclude, I think, that our ancient lyrical poetry was for the most part produced by men who followed what Burns calls " the rhyming trade " as a regular occupation. Mr. Tytler, the historian, says : " There can be no doubt that Scotland from an early period produced multitudes of errant minstrels, who combined the character of the bard and the musician, and, wandering with their harp from castle to castle, sang to the assembled lords and dames those romantic ballads of love and war which formed the popular poetry of the day. It was impossible, indeed, that it could be otherwise. The Gothic tribes which at a very early period possessed themselves of the Lowlands ; the Saxons or Northumbrians who dwelt on the Border ; the Scandinavians or Norwegians who for several centuries maintained possession of the Islands and of Ross and Caithness ; and the Normans, whose original love for romantic fiction was cherished by their residence in France, were all passionately addicted to poetry. They possessed a wild imagination, and a dark and gloomy mythology — they peopled the caves, the woods, the rivers, and the mountains with spirits, elves, giants, and dragons; and are we to wonder that the Scots, a nation in whose veins the blood of all these ancient races is mingled, should at a remote period have evinced an enthusiastic admiration for song and poetry—that the harper was to be found among the officers who composed the personal state of the sovereign, and that the country maintained a privileged race of wandering minstrels, who eagerly seized on the prevailing superstitions and romantic legends, and wove them into rude but sometimes expressive versification, who were welcome guests at the gate of every feudal castle, and beloved by the great body of the people."

The books of the Lord High Treasurer in the reign of James IV. supply evidence of the high estimation in which popular poetry and music were anciently held. From these we find that Blind Harry, the chronicler of Wallace, was a regular pensioner of the gallant monarch who fell at Flodden. They record payments to Wallas, the professional reciter "that tells gests to the king"; to Widerspune, the fowler, that told tales; to two fiddlers, that sung "Graysteel" to the king; to Hog, the tale-teller; to the "menstralls in Linclowden," when the abbey so called was visited by his Sovereign Grace; besides numerous gratuities to harpers, luters, trumpeters, performers on the clairshach and other instruments; also to such notable characters as the broken-backed fiddler in St. Andrews, and the crooked vicar of Drumfries, who sang to the King in Lochmaben. "I remember well," says Mr. Aytoun, "when the mother of the guns, Mons Meg, was brought back with all the honours of the pibroch to the Castle of Edinburgh; but I was not then aware of the fact that before Flodden was fought that venerable piece of ordnance had rolled down the ancient streets of Dunedin, preceded by 'menstralls that playit before mons doun the gate.' I doubt whether the court of good King René of Provence was more minstrel-haunted than that of James IV. of Scotland."

But I must have done with this part of our subject, and hasten to say something more regarding the ballads themselves—those striking and wonderful productions originated and circulated in the manner we have described. Charming they were to our ancestors, and for us their children they still retain an attraction that more regular and polished verse can seldom exercise. "All men," says Professor Wilson, "are antiquaries at the recital of a good old historical or romantic ballad; and a homely word that breathes of the olden time carries back into the past even those who live almost entirely for the present, and who in their ordinary thoughts forget wholly their wild forefathers of the hills and vales, and all that vanished life of peace or tumult, of war or love, and of all the passions that then as now were rife beneath the shepherd's coat of grey as beneath the mail of his feudal lord. O, gentle reader! if ever thou shouldst be wearied to death with Mr. Wordsworth's *Excursion*, take up a volume of *The Minstrelsy of the Scottish Border*, and you will feel your youth renewed. The great Laker speaks of his shepherds eloquently and well, but in the ancient strains we feel that shepherds and herdsmen are themselves speaking. They tell the truth of huts where poor men lie; and narrow and circumscribed as that range of thought and feeling may be, everything is vivid, real, intense, alive, as fixed and stirless as death, or ghastly and sullen as something dying, or eager and wild as that which is recovering life. 'Chevy Chase,' as Sir Philip Sidney said, 'stirs the blood as the sound of a trumpet.' Not one of our great living poets would so speak of Percy or Douglas as has been done by some of the lowly born and obscurely dead. Even Sir Walter, the best of all our civic battle bards, must give in to the old ministrels."

In many instances the ballads were coeval

with the events to which they relate. They
frequently take a dramatic form, and no sooner
did the ministrel get his harp and voice put
into proper trim than he commenced his nar-
rative without any prelude, and sometimes he
hurried into the very middle of the plot, leav-
ing its antecedents to be gathered or guessed
at by his hearers as best they could. He
manifested an unwavering faith in the stories
he told, however marvellous and improbable
they might seem to cold, critical, prosaic minds;
but his audiences, whether made up of gentle
folks or simple, were usually receptive and
sympathetic as well as credulous; and I fancy
he was very rarely challenged for proof, even
when the feats he described seemed no less
superhuman than the miraculous ones attri-
buted to 'The Seven Champions of Christen-
dom.' Usually his heroes and heroines belonged
to the higher classes, thus affording, says
Motherwell, an additional proof of the anti-
quity of the ballads, and that their date "was
anterior to those circumstances that overthrew
the institutions of chivalry and sapped the
foundations of feudal aristocracy, thereby in-
troducing the mixed aspect and form of society
now known in this country."

Of proper names the balladists had a very
restricted stock. Sometimes indeed the hero,
like "the Black Knight" in *Ivanhoe*, appears

upon the stage without any patronymic, and the lady of his love is individualised only by a description of her charms, as in the case of the " Sleeping Beauty " of the well-known fairy tale. William, or Willie, the name which the ministrels hold in most favour, figures in their verse ten times at least for once in which John, James, Thomas, or Patrick is so honoured, while Margaret and Annie receive special prominence in the nomenclature of the gentle sex, Marjorie, Maisry, Jean, and Janet coming next; and, however singular it may seem, the name of which Byron sang, " There is a magic in the name of Mary," and which is now so popular in Scotland, is borne only by one of the ballad heroines.

Notice has already been taken of the sameness in incident and phrase by which many of the poems are characterised, and a few examples of this mannerism may now be introduced. With the old minstrels the Martinmas time was a favourite season, so, though not to the same extent, was the Lammastide. Very often the fair heroine of their tales has a flinty-hearted father or cruel brother, and sometimes seven bauld brethren bent on crossing her plans. When any one wishes a message despatched, a summons is sure to be made for " a bonnie boy," who is promised hose and shoon as a recompence. When the youth sets

off, "the lei licht o' the moon" brightens his
path, or we are told, "It is mirk mirk nicht
and nae star licht;" and it is invariably stated
that—

> When he cam to broken brigs
> He bent his bow and swam,
> And when he cam to grass growin
> He set doun his feet and ran.

On entering in hot haste some bower or
castle to deliver his message, there is usually
some gruff porter to bribe or elude, and before
he can announce his object he is frequently
asked by the owner of the premises—

> Oh is my bigly bower broken,
> Or is my castle won?

or some other similar cause is suggested for the
haste of the messenger; then, as a matter of
course, the boy tells his ingenious interrogator,
in the same set of terms, that his guesses are all
wrong; and next he delivers his real errand,
which, if it be to some bauld baron, and pro-
vokingly unacceptable, the indignant thane
occasionally gives vent to his ire in the vulgar
style of—

> Kepping the table wi' his foot,
> And catching it wi' his knee,
> Till siller cup and mazer dish
> In flinders he gars flee.

Usually when the recipient of a letter reads its first line he indulges in a fit of laughter, but the next puts him into a melting mood— "The saut tear blins his e'e." In order to elucidate the plot a wylie bower-woman, or false nurse, is of great service, and when the betrayed lady upbraids her perfidious dependant, she appeals to her just as a modern mistress would—

> Have I no paid your hire, maiden,
> Or have I no paid your fee?

If, in the tales of blighted love, the heroine dies to-day, her disconsolate swain dies to-morrow, in accordance with his prediction to that effect, and the finale is thus expressed—

> They buried him in St. Mary's kirk,
> And her in St. Mary's quire,
> And out of her grave there grew a red rose,
> And out of the knight's a brier.

When the deserted damsel does not die outright she proclaims a crusade against all coifs and combs, and proscribes the light of coal and candle, that the darkness of her chamber may be in keeping with the desolateness of her heart. Heaven is symbolised by the gillyflower and the birch, night is indicated by the phrase—

> Bells are rung and mass is sung,
>   And a' men bound to bed.

And daybreak is sure to be heralded by the crowing of cocks—a figure that is beautifully diversified in Clerk Saunders when the wandering ghost says—

> O cocks are crowing a merry midnight,
>   I wot the wild-fowls are boding day,
> The psalms of heaven will soon be sung,
>   And I ere now will be missed away.

Sometimes when a difficulty occurs that cannot be solved by ordinary means, a supernatural personage called the Billy Blin turns up at the right moment for that purpose—that is to say if no obliging magpie, parrot, or gay goss-hawk volunteers to explain the mystery.

To the professional rhymer these familiar verses were a source of great convenience; they added to his stock-in-trade, and, being as a rule pithy, expressive, and tuneful, they readily caught hold of the popular ear, which relished them none the less because of their frequent repetition, just as " the music of a hidden brook in the leafy month of June " is, despite of its monotones, never tiresome, but always pleasant.   But the best of the minstrels never based their claims to a hearing on passages borrowed from what was the common property of them all.   They manifested the opulence and individuality of their resources in a rare boldness of thought, couched in words of surpassing beauty, many samples of which are given in the following pages, and they could easily be multiplied.   " Oh were I on Parnassus Hill, and had of Helicon my fill," exclaimed our great national poet; but he found a source of inspiration more suited to his genius than classical Greece could furnish in the old minstrels' fount of song, which, rippling over the hills and dales of his own land, has become to it a perennial heritage.   Ramsay, Scott, Hogg, Tannahill, Cunningham, and Lady Nairne, wooed the Muse, like Burns, in the best sense by studying the old Scottish ballads; and many bards of note belonging to other countries have drawn from them a bias nature-ward and an abiding stimulus.   Being dead, the nameless poets of other days still sing through the medium of their surviving productions, and the numerous songs to which their ballads have given birth.

HISTORICAL AND WARLIKE.

SIR PATRICK SPENS.

PURSUING a long-established custom with our ballad collectors and critics, I give the premier place to the beautiful and affecting metrical tale of Sir Patrick Spens. It is one of the few which has the treacherous sea for its element. Very seldom, indeed, do catastrophes on the ocean figure in the minstrel's verse, though so far back as the reign of Malcolm Canmore a close sea-ward intercourse, not without its usual risks, was kept up between Scottish merchants

and the trading communities of North-Western
Europe.   A few ships of war were also owned
by that monarch, and in the reign of James
IV. the navy of "the north countrie" became
sufficiently formidable to keep that of Eng-
land in check, when the two nations were at
war with each other.   But the disaster de-
scribed and bewailed in the old ballad before
us occurred neither to trading cruiser nor
ship of war, but to the grand State vessel
which conveyed Margaret, daughter of Alex-
ander III., to Norway, as the affianced bride of
its sovereign, King Eric.   Alexander, sitting
in Dunfermline town, " drinking the blude-
red wine," expresses a wish to obtain the
services of " a skeely skipper to sail this ship
of mine "—

> Then up and spak an eldern knyght,
>   Sat at the king's richt knee :
> " Sir Patrick Spens is the best sailor
>   That ever sailed the sea."

In due course Sir Patrick, while " walking
on the strand," received a holograph letter
from his royal master, which he read thus :—

> To Norroway, to Norroway,
>   To Norroway o'er the faem,
> The king's daughter to Norroway,
>   It 's thou maun tak her hame.

The first feeling of the distinguished skipper was one of joy because of his being intrusted with such an important mission ; but the risks it involved elicited from him a manifestation of regret ; the winter, which had set in with its storms, rendering the navigation of the North Sea more than usually perilous—

> The first word that Sir Patrick read,
>   Sae loud, loud laughéd he ;
> The neist word that Sir Patrick read,
>   The tear blinded his e'e.

Nevertheless he readily responded to the royal summons ; any reluctance he felt being due, I fancy, to the dread that some evil might befall the fair young princess who was to be placed under his charge. Fortunately no stormy billows were encountered by the vessel, and, favoured by propitious breezes, its precious royal freight was borne to her destination in safety. Possibly the minstrel would in his next verses have introduced a sort of epithalamium, however brief and rude, had it not been that the burden of a great sorrow lay heavily upon his mind, keeping it out of tune with the bells that rung out merrily in honour of the royal nuptials. Not a word does he say about the marriage. He lets us know, however, that the Scandinavian nobles hastened the departure of the Scottish captain by complaining churlishly that King Eric's purse had been heavily drawn upon for the entertainment of the foreigners.   In blunt sailor-like style Sir Patrick annihilated the falsehood—

" Ye lee, ye lee, ye leers loud,
    Sae loud 's I hear ye lee,

" For I brocht as much o' the white monie
    As gane my men and me,
And a half-fu' o' the gude red gowd
    Out owre the sea wi' me."

Make ready at once for the homeward voyage, we can abide no longer here after having been so vilely traduced ; and the Scottish knight made arrangements accordingly, though the weather had taken an unfavourable turn, and the signal of a pending tempest had been hoisted in the heavens.

" Be 't wind or weet, be 't snaw or sleet,
    Our ship shall sail the morn."

One of Sir Patrick's men ventured to tell him of the woful omen, but the warning fell unheeded—

" I saw the new moon, late yestreen,
    Wi' the auld moon in her airm ; "

and sure enough, when three leagues from land, the threatened hurricane overtook the doomed vessel: "The ropes they brak, and the top-masts lap," and the billows struck her mercilessly, "till a' her sides were torn." Hitherto the captain had with his own hand steered the ship, but finding she could not possibly keep afloat much longer, he intrusted the helm to "a gude sailor," and proceeded to climb the tall top-mast in the vain hope of descrying some sheltering haven or hospitable shore within reach.

He hadna gane a step, a step,
    A step but barely ane,
When a bolt flew oot o' the goodly ship,
    And the saut sea it cam in.

Obeying the captain's orders, the crew

Fetched a wab o' the silken claith,
    Anither o' the twine,
And wapped them into the gude ship's side,
    But aye the sea cam in.

O laith, laith were our gude Scots lords
    To weet their cork-heeled shoon,
But lang ere a' the play was played
    They wat their heads abune.

And mony were the feather-beds
  That floated on the faem,
And mony war the gude lords' sons
  That never mair cam hame.

O lang, lang may the ladies sit
  Wi' their fans into their hand,
Or e'er they see Sir Patrick Spens
  Come sailing to the strand !

And lang, lang may the maidens sit
  Wi' their gowd kames in their hair,
A-waiting for their ain dear loves,
  For them they 'll see nae mair.

Half owre, half owre to Aberdour
  It 's fifty fathoms deep,
And there lies good Sir Patrick Spens,
  Wi' the Scots lords at his feet.

Professor Aytoun, whose version of the
ballad I have followed in preference to that
of Sir Walter Scott, states that in the little
island of Papa Stronsay, Orcadia, there is a
large grave or tumulus which has been known
to the inhabitants from time immemorial as
the grave of Sir Patrick Spens. " Is it then,"
he asks, " a forced conjecture that the ship-
wreck took place off the iron-bound coast of
the northern islands ? Half over to Aberdour
signifies nothing more than that the vessel
went half-way between Norway and the port
of embarkation."

GUDE WALLACE.

The exploits of Sir William Wallace have been well sung by Blind Harry, and they were not overlooked by other minstrels. In all likelihood the doughty doings of the Deliverer of Scotland long formed a stock theme for singers, harpers, and reciters. Scarcely could it have been otherwise. The great saviour of his country, the man "who rescued Scotland thrys" from the galling English yoke, and who sealed his patriotism with his blood, must have waked up the soul of Scottish song; and had the harp of the north been silent, methinks the very stones would have become articulate—the very hills and dales which he redeemed to freedom would have become vocal with his praise. Few ballads however, by nameless composers, on this great theme have been preserved, and of these the one I am about to notice is the best. Blind Harry records the incidents on which it is founded, laying the scene of them in the vicinity of Lochmaben.

In the opening verses we find the hero reduced to dreadful straits. The Southrons, after being driven out of the kingdom, have returned in greater force than before, and so overrun the land that the patriot band are

sore scattered, and their chief is in perpetual
danger of being taken by the enemy, and is
exposed to every hardship. Weakened by
fatigue and hunger, he hies from his hiding-
place towards a neighbouring town, and
accosting "a weel-faured maid" washing her
hands in a running stream—it may be the
Dryfe or the Annan—requested to hear from
her the news of the day. The answer is, that
the only tidings she had heard was that
fifteen Englishmen were in the hostelry near
by, on the look-out for Wallace. He expresses
a wish to go down and see the strangers, but
mentions as a hindrance the emptiness of his
pouch ; and with that the liberal lass, charmed,
we suppose, by the winsome manner of the
belted knight, hands him out half-a-crown to
pay his lawin'. Wallace, thus supplied with
needful cash, meets next with "a beggar
bold," who confirms the previous news, and
readily lends his clouted cloak to the hero,
under cover of which the latter goes to the
inn, having first, however, supplied himself
with a trusty staff torn from a wayside thicket.
In the guise of a puir, feckless auld man, he
asks the English leader for charity, when the
following question is put to him :—

" Whaur were ye born, ye crooked carle ?
Whaur were ye born, in what countrie ? "

The answer is " Fair Scotland," which induces
the captain to reason thus : Here is a wander-
ing Scotch beggar, who probably, in ranging
up and down, knows something as to the
whereabouts of Wallace. I must sound him
on the subject, and, if need be, secure his
services by a tempting bait. He further
questions the seeming mendicant, and, as the
result of their brief conference, agrees to pay
him £50 of white money for a sight of the
traitor. Nowhere have we a better illustra-
tion of the reckless courage and herculean
prowess of Wallace wight than is forthwith
narrated. He was, be it remembered, weakened
by hunger and fatigue, but mark what doughty
deeds followed wordy parle ; and notice, by
the way, how, with true Caledonian shrewd-
ness, Wallace stipulates that the money he is
about to win shall be true and not counter-
feit—

"Tell down your monie," said Willie
    Wallace,
" Tell down your monie, if it be gude,
For I'm sure I hae it in my power,
  And I never had a better bode.

"Tell down your monie, if it be gude,
  And let us see if it be fine,
For I 'm sure I hae it in my power
  To bring the traitor Wallace in."

The monie was told down on the table,
  Silver white of pounds fiftie.
" Now here I stand," said Willie Wallace,
  " And what hae ye got to say to me ? "

He fell'd the captain where he stood,
  Wi' a downright straik upon the floor,
He slew the rest around the room,
  And speer'd gin there was any more.

Not a single Englishman was to be seen in
the house, and the famishing hero supposed
he might now indulge in a dinner with
safety—

" Come, cover the table," quo' Willie Wallace,
  " Come, cover the table now and wi' haste.
For it will sune be three lang days
  Sin I a bit o' meat did taste."

But though mine host readily obeyed the
summons by parading a plentiful feast, before
a particle of it had been put to the lips of his
guest, other fifteen Englishmen, who had been
waiting at a distance outside, hurried in to
ascertain the fate of their comrades, and also
to share it.   Wallace, reinforced by the gude-
man of the house, assailed them with renewed
strength, and with such effect that none
escaped to tell the tale :—

He put his faes in sic a swither,
    That five o' them he stickit dead,
Five o' them he drowned in the river,
    And five he hung in the West-muir wood.

Now he is off to the water-side,
    Where the maid was washing tenderlie:
" Now by my sooth," said the Gude Wallace,
    " It's been a sair day's wark to me."

He put his hand into his pocket,
    And he has paid out twenty pound ;
Says, " Tak ye that, ye weel-faured maid,
    For the gude luck o' your half-crown."

Full five-and-twenty men he slew,
    And five he hanged upon a grain ;
In the morn he sat with his merry men a',
    Within Lochmaben toun at dine.

BATTLE OF OTTERBURN.

The conflicts between the Scots and " their auld enemies," the English, are picturesquely mirrored in the lays of the old minstrels. One of the principal of these engagements was the Battle of Otterburn, to which ample justice has been done by a forgotten bard. Froissart tells us in his graphic narrative that in 1387 James, Earl of Douglas, with his brother, the Earl of Murray, invaded Northumberland at the head of 3000 men, whilst the Earls of Fife and Strathearn, sons of the Scottish king, ravaged the western borders of England with a still more numerous army. Douglas penetrated as far as Newcastle, where Henry Percy, the redoubted Hotspur, lay in garrison. A personal encounter took place between the champions, which is forcibly described by the balladist. Percy having, in answer to a question from Douglas, stated that he was lord, and his wife the lady, of the castle, the Scottish chief said—

> " If thou 'rt the lord of this castel,
>   Come down and fight wi' me,
> For ere I cross the Border fells
>   The tane o' us shall dee."

> He took a lang spear in his hand.
>   Shod with the metal free,
> And forth to meet the Douglas then,
>   He rade richt furiouslie.

> But oh, how pale his lady looked
>   Frae aff' the castle wa',
> When down before the Scottish spear
>   She saw proud Percy fa'.

Douglas, according to the balladist, declared that had they been alone, and Percy's men not interfered, he would have had him flesh and fell ; and, says Froissart, he took Percy's lance, with the pennon attached to it, and shaking it aloft, swore he would carry it as spoil into Scotland, and plant it upon his castle of Dalkeith. "That," answered Percy, "shall thou never;" and the chivalrous Douglas, to give his enemy an opportunity of redeeming the pennon and recovering his lost honour, agreed to meet him ere three days elapsed at Otterburn, distant about thirty-two miles from Newcastle. Accordingly, Hotspur, having collected his men from the marches, so as to make up a larger force than that under Douglas, attacked the Scottish camp under cover of night. An engagement took place which proved to be one of the most desperate on record. It terminated in the defeat of the English, but the triumph was dearly purchased, Douglas falling mortally wounded when the combat was at its crisis. The opening incidents are beautifully depicted in the ballad :—

> They lichted high on Otterburn,
>   Upon the bent sae brown,
> They lichted high on Otterburn,
>   And pitched their pallions down.

> And he that had a bonnie boy,
>   He sent his horse to grass,
> And he that had not a bonnie boy,
>   His ain servant he was.

Then up and spak a little boy,
  Was near of Douglas kin,
" Methink I see an English host
  Come brankin us upon.

" Nine wargangs bearing broad and wide,
  Seven banners bearing high,
It wad do ony living gude
  To see their colours fly."

" If this be true, my little boy,
  That thou tells unto me,
The brawest bower o' the Ottertowre
  Shall be thy morning fee.

" But I hae dreamed a dreary dream,
  Ayont the Isle of Skye
I saw a dead man win a fight,
  And I think that man was I."

He belted on his gude braid sword,
  And to the field he ran,
But he forgot the hewmont strong
  That should have kept his brain.

Deeply pathetic is the scene which ensues
on the fall of Douglas. His " ae dear sister's
son," having bent down beside his gory bed,

" My nephew gude," the Douglas said,
  " What recks the death of ane,
Last night I dreamed a dreary dream,
  And I ken the day's my ain.

"My wound is deep, I fain wad sleep;
    Take thou the vanguard of the three,
And hide me by the bracken bush
    That grows on yonder lily lea.

"O bury me by the bracken bush,
    Beneath the blooming breer,
Let never living mortal ken
    That a kindly Scot lies here."

He lifted up that noble lord,
    With the saut tear in his 'ee,
And he hid him by the bracken bush,
    That his merry men might not see.

The fight went on with unabated vigour—

The Gordons gay, in English blude
    They wat their hose and shoon,
The Lindsays flew like fire about,
    Till all the fray was done.

It ended, as we have said, in the thorough
defeat of the Southrons; and Sir Hugh
Montgomery, having made Hotspur prisoner,
carried him to Scotland, and, by way of ran-
som, made him pay for the building of Penorn
Castle, in the county of Ayr.

EDOM O' GORDON.

This ballad is replete with tragical effects, all very touchingly evolved. It is based on real incidents which occurred after the dethronement of Queen Mary, and while her cause, though hopeless, was upheld by Lord Huntly and other nobles. Adam, or Edom Gordon, brother of the Earl, slew Arthur Forbes in one of his ravaging forays. Afterwards, he marched a force against the tower of Rodes in Berwickshire that belonged to Alexander Forbes, brother of Arthur, an adherent of Mary's son, King James. Gordon summoned the house to surrender at a time when, as he well knew, its custodian was absent. Thereupon Lady Forbes held parley with Gordon from the upper battlements,

> To see if by her fair speeches,
> She could wi' him agree.

A comely person, her charms captivated the rough warrior, and he engaged to spare her and her children on terms which no true lady could accept. Her answer was decisive—

> "I winna come doon, ye fause Gordon,
> I winna come doon to thee,
> I winna forsake my ain dear lord,
> That is sae far frae me."

But Edom, in whose heart fell hate was rapidly taking the place of tumultuous lust, gave the lady final warning in the following terms :—

> " Gie owre your house, ye lady fair,
>   Gie owre your house to me,
> Or I shall burn yoursel' therein,
>   But and your babies three."

The heroine's retort was one of deeds, not words, and daringly defiant. Turning to her man Glaud, she called for pistol and gun, telling him that unless she pierced " the bluidy butcher's heart, we a' shall be undone ;" a bullet from her firelock missed its aim, but grazing the fause Gordon's knee, made him " wud wi' dule and ire," and precipitated the catastrophe, fell treachery on the part of a retainer contributing to its fulfilment. Retiring with her children three and a few vassals to a remote portion of the house, she cherished a hope that they might be able to keep themselves unharmed by the flames that were enveloping the lower storey, and that haply her husband might appear in time to effect their full deliverance. Many a wistful look was cast by the poor lady over dale and down for her good lord. " He cometh not," she said, despairingly. And see ! the false knave already referred to is at work removing a stone from the protecting wall, and through the orifice thus formed streams the devouring element with resistless speed ! Reproachfully she thus addressed the traitor :—

> "Wae worth, wae worth ye, Jock, my man,
>   I paid ye weel your fee ;
> Why pu' ye oot the grund-wa' stane,
>   Lets in the reek to me ?

> "And e'en wae worth ye, Jock, my man,
>   I paid ye weel your hire ;
> Why pu' ye oot the grund-wa' stane,
>   To me lets in the fire ?"

" Bought over by the enemy" was the only explanation which the heartless wretch could give. Even yet, perhaps, her case was not thoroughly hopeless. Possibly if she had commissioned the traitor to tell Gordon that for her children's sake she was ready to submit to his foul embrace, she and they might have been "snatched as brands from the burning." But honour was dearer to her than life, and proof even to the pleadings of those for whose sake she would have sacrificed everything save fidelity to her absent lord. How piteously they did plead, the youngest child sitting on the nurse's knee, alternating its screams with the convulsive cry—

" O mother dear, gie owre this house,
  For the reek it smothers me."

But the mother, with the courage of a martyr
at the stake, resisted the appeal, and could
only say—

" I wad gie a' my gowd, my bairn,
  Sae wad I a' my fee,
For ae blast o' the westlin wind,
  To blaw the reek frae thee."

A request then made by her grown-up daugh-
ter—

" O row me in a pair o' sheets,
  And tow me owre the wa',"

was readily complied with ; but ere the dainty
little maiden touched the ground the spear of
the monster Gordon was placed by him in
such a position that it pierced her through,
with fatal results.

O bonnie, bonnie was her mouth,
  And cherry were her cheeks,
And clear, clear was her yellow hair,
  Whereon the red blude dreeps.

When Edom o' Gordon surveyed his victim
he was filled with remorse, her marvellous
beauty rendering his feelings increasingly
bitter.

Then wi' his spear he turned her owre—
  O gin her face was wan;
He said, "You are the first that e'er
  I wished alive again."

He turned her owre and owre again—
  O gin her skin was white;
" I micht hae spared that bonnie face,
  To hae been some man's delight.

" Busk and boun, my merrie men a',
  For ill dooms do I guess,
I canna look on that bonnie face,
  As it lies on the grass."

While Gordon and his followers rode off,
they could see the house of the Rodes swathed
in flame, and probably they heard, too, the
"wild mother scream o'er her perishing
brood" from its burning walls, after she had
kissed her children twain for the last time,
and told them in half-stifled tones, "Bairns,
we been but dead."

" Put on, put on, my wightie men,
  So fast as ye can drie,
For he that is hinmost o' the thrang
  Shall ne'er get gude o' me."

These words were addressed by Alexander
Forbes to his followers when, on returning
home, he was appalled by seeing his castle
all a-flame.

> Then some they rade, and some they ran,
>   Fu' fast out owre the bent,
> But ere the foremost could win up,
>   Baith lady and babes were brent.

" He wrang his hands, he rent his hair"; then, bent on a bloody reprisal, he hurried after the destroyer of his household. One version of the ballad states that Forbes overtook Gordon and instantly despatched him; another says that all but five of Edom's fifty followers shared his fate, and adds a terrible sequel to the tale that is all through awfully tragical. After Forbes had glutted his vengeance, life had nothing left worth living for. Returning to the still burning castle, he sought out the ashes of his wife and children, and, wishing to be with his dear ones in death,

> At last into the flames he ran,
>   And bade the world adieu.

Regarding this finale, which is quite in the style of the old minstrels, history is silent; but it bears testimony to the other leading incidents. According to Spottiswoode, Lady Forbes, her children and servants, twenty-seven persons in all, perished in the flames that turned into a blackened ruin the doomed house of Rodes.

LORD MAXWELL'S GOOD-NIGHT.

A considerable extent of Dumfriesshire history is covered by this well-known ballad. It recalls the leading incidents of a feud between the Border houses of Maxwell and Johnstone that lasted for several generations, during which, says Sir Walter Scott, " each lost two chieftains—one dying of a broken heart, one on the field of battle, one by assassination, and one by the sword of the executioner."

> " Adieu ! madame, my mother dear,
>   But and my sisters three ;
> Adieu ! fair Robert of Orchardstane,
>   My heart is wae for thee.
>
> Adieu ! the lily and the rose,
>   The primrose fair to see ;
> Adieu ! my ladye, and only joy,
>   For I may not stay with thee."

With these touching words John, the ninth Lord Maxwell, began the farewell address which bears his name. Why should he leave wife, mother, sisters three, and the Knight of Orchardstane, who was more than a brother to him ? For cogent reasons, which he proceeds to set forth.

" Though I hae slain the Lord Johnstone,
   What care I for their feid ?
My noble mind their wrath disdains,
   He was my father's deid.

" Both night and day I laboured oft
   Of him avenged to be ;
But now I 've got what lang I sought,
   And I may not stay with thee."

Had the slaughter of the Laird of Johnstone here spoken of been in the heat of battle, or in a personal duel fairly conducted, Maxwell would have been under no necessity for quitting Scotland ; but the deed of blood was treacherously accomplished during a private interview held between the two barons for the ostensible purpose of settling their family quarrel in peace. It was at the famous clan battle of Dryfe Sands, fought on the 6th of December, 1593, which terminated in the utter defeat of the Nithsdale force, that its leader, the eighth Lord Maxwell, lost his life. When retreating from the field the unfortunate nobleman was thrown from his horse and despatched by an Annandale trooper, though he offered to submit without resistance ; hence the desire for vengeance cherished by his son. After the lapse of nearly fifteen years, during which the two chieftains continued at enmity,

the tryst above referred to took place. Lord
Maxwell was accompanied by his cousin, Sir
Robert Maxwell of Orchardstane or Spottes,
and another relative of evil repute, Charles
Maxwell; the Laird of Johnstone having for his
supporter a near kinsman, William Johnstone
of Lockerbie. " They met on horseback," says
Calderwood the historian, " and salute each
other heartily in outward show, and went
apart to confer together. While Johnstone
and Maxwell are conferring apart, Maxwell's
second (Charles Maxwell) began to quarrel
Johnstone's second, and shot a pistolet at
him, whereupon he fell. Johnstone, hearing
the shot, cried 'Treason!' and riding from
Maxwell to the two gentlemen to understand
what the matter meant, Maxwell shooteth him
behind the back. So Johnstone fell, and died
of the shot." For another publication I drew
up an account of this deplorable tragedy,
based upon evidence given at the trial of
Lord Maxwell, a few lines from which may
be here introduced. After Johnstone shouted
" Murder! treason!" his chief, " hearing the
alarming cry, turns round to ride back ; so does
Lord Maxwell, the latter at the same time
drawing a pistol and preparing to take aim at
Sir James. 'Fie! my lord,' cries Sir Robert
Maxwell in terror, ' mak not yourself a traitor
and me both.' 'Upbraid me not,' answers

his lordship, ' I am wyteless '; yet he follows the unsuspecting Laird of Johnstone—fires—the shot takes fatal effect—for a minute or more the dying man retains his seat—then the weak old nag below him founders—its girths give way—prone to the earth falls the ill-fated chief, treacherously slain in the flower of his age—life's sands ebbing rapidly away. His faithful friend vainly endeavours to get him borne off on his own powerful steed. While thus employed, Charles Maxwell, with superfluous malignity, fires another pistol at the bleeding victim, who, after dolefully exclaiming, ' I am deceived,' and fervently praying, ' Lord have mercy on me! Christ have mercy on me!' breathes his last, and is beyond the reach of the fiendish hate that plotted his ruin, and the help of the strong human love which his kinsman manifests by ineffectual sobs and tears."

The murder of Johnstone under these circumstances occasioned a most painful sensation throughout Annandale; his kinsmen demanded life for life, and the Government felt under the necessity of employing all the machinery of the law in order to bring the criminal to justice. Maxwell narrowly escaped capture on several occasions; and, with the view of baffling his pursuers, fled to France, the supposed feelings of the fugitive

in leaving home and friends receiving beauti-
ful expression in the ballad under notice.

> "Adieu! Dumfries, my proper place,
>   But and Carlaverock fair;
> Adieu! my castle of the Thrieve,
>   Wi' a' my buildings there.
>
> Adieu! Lochmaben's gates sae fair,
>   The Langholm holm where birks there be;
> Adieu! my ladye, and only joy,
>   For I may not stay with thee."
>
> "Lord of the land," that ladye said,
>   "O wad ye go wi' me
> Unto my brother's stately tower,
>   Where safest ye may be!
>
> Where Hamiltons and Douglas baith
>   Shall rise to succour thee."
> "Thanks for thy kindness, fair my dame,
>   But I may not stay with thee."

Maxwell must needs depart. He felt that
neither the princely Hamiltons (a daughter
of whose house he had married) nor yet
the doughty Douglases, to whom he was also
related, could confer upon him adequate pro-
tection; and so

> The wind was fair, the ship was clear,
>   The good Lord went away,
> The most part of his friends were there
>   To give him a fair convey.

They drank the wine, they didna spare.
　　Even in that gude Lord's sight ;
Sae now he 's ower the flood sae grey,
　　And Lord Maxwell has ta'en his good-night.

Good-night ! Good-night !　Let the adieu of the Nithsdale chief be for evermore, lest by recalling it evil days, darkened and embittered by the shadow of death, fall to his lot—to be shortened only by the axe of the executioner. But the unhappy exile, wearied with wandering on a foreign strand, resolved at whatever risk to see the land of his birth and love once more.　He ventured back to it after an absence of four years.　Offered an asylum in Castle Sinclair by his wife's cousin, the Earl of Caithness, he fled thither ; but that nobleman, wishing to curry favour with the King, surrendered him to the officers of the law, and from that day forth he stood face to face with death.　Thus, by a singular act of retribution, the man who had slaughtered the Annandale chief under trust was, while under trust, betrayed by his own near relative to the Government.　Good-night ! once again—this time for ever and ever !　Oh how overwhelmingly bitter must have been Lord Maxwell's experience when from the scaffold, on the 21st of May, 1613, he took his long and last farewell of earth and all it contained, of his nearest and dearest, more precious to him than the life itself which he was about to lose. His fate was deplored by a host of mourners, many of whom viewed his crime as a legitimate piece of feudal revenge. Throughout Nithsdale, Eskdale, and the district watered by the Galloway Dee it excited the deepest sorrow and regret. In the eyes of his own kinsmen Maxwell was no malefactor: they sorrowed for him as one who had been unfortunate, who had during his exile expiated his offences, and to whom the clemency of the Crown ought to have been extended. He was their chief, the representative of an ancient and illustrious house, who, whatever might have been his faults to others, still merited their affection. How could they therefore do otherwise than lament his fate? His execution is not mentioned by the old minstrel, as that took place after the date of his ballad. Had he made it the theme of a second poem he would perhaps have given adequate expression to the general sorrow that it awakened; and if so, " Lord Maxwell's Good-Night " would have had a fitting sequel in Lord Maxwell's Dirge.

When a great modern minstrel, Lord Byron, as " Childe Harold " left England on his famous " Pilgrimage," he seized his harp, and, with the lay of the old Scottish lyrist ring-

ing in his ears, "he tuned his farewell in the
dim twilight," beginning his beautiful and
affecting ballad thus—

> Adieu, adieu ! My native shore
>   Fades o'er the waters blue ;
> The night-winds sigh, the breakers roar,
>   And shrieks the wild sea-mew.
>
> Yon sun that sets upon the sea
>   We follow in his flight ;
> Farewell awhile to him and thee,
>   My native land, Good-Night !

THE BURNING OF FRENDRAUGHT.

Frendraught Tower, Deeside, was destroyed
by fire, with six of its occupiers, under ex-
tremely tragical circumstances in 1630. It
was a tall square keep of three storeys, each
having one apartment. The lowest storey was
of massive stone, in the vaulted roof of which
there was an aperture allowing communica-
tion by ladders with the second storey, and
both it and the third were thinner in the
walls, and timber-panelled. To this pile, day-
light was admitted through narrow loops of
windows protected by heavy iron stanchions ;
both inside and out wearing anything but a
cheerful aspect. This explanation will enable

the reader to understand the peculiar straits to which the inmates of the tower were reduced when it became suddenly enveloped in flames soon after midnight, whilst they were all fast asleep, and egress could not be obtained by either the doors or windows. This fell catastrophe is the theme of a vigorous old ballad, the author of which states that the fire was wilfully raised by the owner of the building, Crichton of Frendraught, for the purpose of dealing vengeance upon Gordon of Rothiemay, his chief guest, with whom he had previously been at deadly feud. History, however, does not place this view beyond doubt, even though judicial proceedings were instituted by the Government for the purpose of clearing up the mystery. A writer who has devoted much pains in trying to unravel it, says, "After the lapse of more than two hundred and fifty years, the affair remains in as impenetrable obscurity as it was at the first." [1] Between Crichton and Gordon "there fell oot a great dispute," and at a battle which ensued, the latter lost his life. The Marquis of Huntly, their feudal superior, and popularly termed the Gudeman of the Bog, imposed a heavy fine upon Crichton, which, when paid, was given as a solatium to the widow. Soon afterwards, Frendraught had

[1] Charles Rampini, in the *Scottish Review*, July, 1887, p. 163.

another quarrel on hand, which led to another
fight, in which James Leslie was severely
wounded. Leslie's father, the old Laird of
Pitcaple, hied away to Huntly at the head of
thirty horsemen, and, having found him at his
castle, Bog o' Gicht, he threw himself on his
protection. The Marquis received his visitor
kindly, and gave him hospitable entertain-
ment. But Frendraught had stolen a march
upon Pitcaple. Having arrived at Bog before
him, he gave his version of the affray to his
over-lord, who, concluding that young Leslie
had been wounded in a fair encounter, felt
that he could not in justice subject his anta-
gonist to any punishment, pecuniary or other-
wise. Pitcaple was indignant when the Mar-
quis intimated this conclusion to him, and
left Bog, threatening vengeance against the
assailant of his son. By way of precaution,
Huntly provided a strong escort for Fren-
draught, giving the command of it to his own
son, John, Viscount Melgum, a lad of twenty-
four, but already married and a father, his wife
having been " bonnie Sophia Hay," a daughter
of the Earl of Errol. Curiously enough, it so
happened that John Gordon, whose father
had been slain by Crichton, was also at Bog;
and he, too, as if he had forgotten the past,
joined the cavalcade, and proceeded with his
father's old enemy to his residence of Fren-

draught Tower. There a luxurious feast awaited the party; and after it had been partaken of, Melgum and his friends rose to return to Bog. But Lady Frendraught and her husband insisted that they should remain all night—

When steeds were saddled and weel bridled,
    And ready for to ride,
Then out came her and fause Frendraught,
    Inviting them to bide.

Said, " Stay this nicht until we sup,
    The morn until we dine ;
'Twill be a token of good gremont
    'Twixt your good lord and mine."

So, to quote the historian Spalding, " they supped merrily and went to bed joyfully." Melgum was lodged in Frendraught's own sleeping room, the bed of which was placed right above the opening in the vaulted chamber, the pages receiving accommodation in the same apartment as their master. Rothiemay and his suite lay in the room above, while the uppermost one was occupied by George Chalmers of North, Captain Rollock, and another of the Viscount's servants. About the " midnight hour, this dolorous tower" took fire " in ane clap," and the flames obtained such a sudden mastery, that all the guests "were cruelly burned and tormented to death, without help or relief: the Laird of Frendraught, his lady, and whole household, looking on without moving or stirring to deliver them from the fury of this fearful fire, as was reported." This is Spalding's statement, based on hearsay evidence. He agrees with the anonymous minstrel in attributing the origin of the fire to the owner of the Tower, and evidently supposed that the "clap" which startled the sleepers was produced by an explosion of gunpowder. According to the balladist, "good Lord John and Rothiemay, in one chamber were laid"; and

> They had not long cast off their clothes,
>   And were but new asleep,
> When the weary smoke began to rise
>   Likewise the scorching heat.
>
> "O waken, waken, Rothiemay,
>   O waken, brother dear,
> And turn ye to our Saviour,
>   There is strong treason here."

Dressing themselves hurriedly, they then vainly tried to open the doors and windows. "Wae to the hands put in the stanchions," cried Gordon, despairingly, "for out we'll never win."

When he stood at the wire window,
  Most doleful to be seen,
He did espy her, Lady Frendraught,
  Who stood upon the green ;

Cried, " Mercy, mercy ! Lady Frendraught.
  Will ye not sink for sin ?
For first your husband killed my father,
  And now you burn his son ! "

Oh then outspoke her, Lady Frendraught,
  And loudly did she cry,
" It were great pity for good Lord John,
  But none for Rothiemay.

" But the keys are casten in the deep draw-
    well,
  Ye cannot get away."

Though Melgum's servants were also cooped
up in the burning hold, the balladist repre-
sents one of them, George Gordon, as being
outside, and shouting out—

" O loup ! O loup ! my dear master,
  O loup ! and come to me,
I 'll catch ye in my armis twa.
  One foot I will not flee."

Never mind Rothiemay, the servant further
urged, leave him to his fate, and look after
your own safety.   But the young lord, who

appears to have had a great affection for his older companion, replied heroically—

> " The fish shall never swim the flood,
>   Nor corn grow through the clay,
> If the fiercest fire that ever was kindled,
>   Twine me and Rothiemay."

In the verses of the minstrel, Melgum appears as the central figure—as the sufferer whose fate was the most to be deplored; and the plaint imputed to him as he is gradually calcined by the consuming flames is terrific in its literalism, and sufficient to move a heart of stone :—

> " My eyes are southering in my head,
>   My flesh roasting also,
> My bowels are boiling with my blood !
>   Isna that an awful woe ?

> " So I cannot loup, I cannot come,
>   I cannot loup to thee,
> My earthly part is all consumed,
>   My spirit but speaks to thee."

But even when the poor young Lord's heart and flesh failed under the merciless torture of the furnace, he thought of home— of the wife there, that was so soon to be a widow.

" Take here the rings frae my fingers,
  That are so long and small,
And give them to my lady fair,
  Where she sits in her hall."

By a stretch of poetic licence the Countess
herself is brought upon the scene—

Wringing her hands, tearing her hair,
  His lady, she was seen
Calling unto his servant Gordon,
  As he stood on the green,

" O wae be to you, George Gordon,
  An ill death may ye dee,
Sae safe and sound as ye stan' there,
  And my lord bereaved frae me."

Gordon vindicates himself by stating what
he had done to save the Viscount.   Inconsol-
able was the lady, driven frantic, even to
madness, by the loss she had sustained.

Sophia Hay, Sophia Hay,
  O bonnie Sophia was her name,
Her waiting-maid put on her clothes,
  But I wat she tore them off again.

The closing incidents at the Tower are thus
recorded by Spalding. " The Viscount, taking
his rings from his fingers, and flinging them
through the bars, desired that they should

be conveyed to his young wife. Then commending her and his child to God, and ' often tymes crying mercy at God's handis for thair synis,' he and Rothiemay, clasped in each other arms, ' cheerfully suffered this cruel martyrdom.' " Such, says Burton, was the awful event " which has to the northern peasant as distinct and tragic a place in history as the Sicilian vespers on the night of St. Bartholomew may have for those whose historical horizon is wider." On the morning after the catastrophe, Lady Frendraught, who was a cousin of Huntly's, travelled to Bog o' Gicht, accompanied by a single page, and asked to see her kinsman ; but the news of the terrible fire had preceded her arrival, and he refused to grant her an interview. By order of the Marquis the bones and ashes of the victims were collected, the remains of each placed in a separate coffin, " six kistis in the haill," and decently buried in the kirk of Gartly.

Dreadful though the tragedy was in itself, its after results to the parties mixed up with it were almost equally heart-rending. " Huntly's last years were embittered—and, perhaps, his death accelerated—by the terrors and annoyances it entailed upon him. It ruined Frendraught, both pecuniarily and socially, and exposed his wife to unmerited insults,"[1] though there is good reason for believing that popular rumour, which charged them with originating the fire, was at fault. Pitcaple also fell under suspicion, but without sufficient proof. A scapegoat for judicial vengeance was called for, however, and found in the person of John Meldrum of Reidhill, Pitcaple's brother-in-law, who, on most inadequate evidence, was convicted of having fired the tower by means of "powder, pik, brumstane, flax, and other combustabill matter" placed by him in its vault, and was adjudged to be hanged, and his goods and lands confiscated to the Crown; which merciless sentence was duly carried into effect.

[1] Article in *Scottish Review*, July, 1887, p. 157.

PART SECOND.

BORDER AND WARLIKE.

JOHNNIE ARMSTRONG.

I SHALL now take a group of Border ballads, beginning with Johnnie Armstrong—not quite so famous as Robin Hood, "the English ballad-singer's joy;" yet Johnnie, the freebooting laird of Gilnockie, earned a great amount of notoriety in his day, and he is the hero of at least two ancient ditties, one of which must have been composed by a minstrel of great poetic skill. Pitscottie tells us that in the reign of James V. Johnnie was the most redoubted chief that had lived on either side of the Marches for a long period. " He rode ever with twenty-four able gentlemen, well horsed; yet he never molested any Scottish man ; but it is said that from the Borders to Newcastle every man, of whatsomever estate, paid him tribute to be free of his trouble." The King, having resolved to punish all habitual law-breakers, and "make the rash bush keep the cow," Johnnie sought, without success, to obtain forgiveness for his past offences, and secure the royal favour. If the ballad is to be relied upon, Johnnie was entrapped by "a loving letter" from King James, inviting him to a conference. Armstrong, on marching off to the place of tryst, accompanied by two score retainers, all unarmed, in accordance with a condition imposed by the King, the ladies on the Langholm houm, looking "frae their loft windows," prayerfully ejaculated, "God bring our men weel back again." The inexorable monarch had, however, resolved that they should never see Gilnockie or fair Eskdalemore.

> When Johnnie cam before the King,
>   Wi' a' his men sae brave to see,
> The King he moved his bonnet to him,
>   He weened he was a king as well as he.

Armstrong, after announcing his name, prayed that he and his "loyal men" might receive grace at the hands of their sovereign liege. The King replied that he had never yet granted a traitor his life, and was not going to alter his policy by pardoning such "a traitor strang" as Johnnie Armstrong. Not being tired of life, the suppliant pleaded hard on behalf of himself and his attendants, appealing less to the clemency than the cupidity of the King. Armstrong declared his readiness to give him "four-and-twenty milk-white steeds,"

"With as meikle gude English gelt,
    As four o' their braid backs can bear."

James, still remaining unmollified, the outlaw threw into his offer "gude four-and-twenty ganging mills;"

"And as meikle gude red wheat
    As a' their happers dow to bear."

"Away, away, thou traitor strang!
    Oot o' my sicht sune mayst thou be,"

reiterated the monarch.

"Grant me my life, my liege, my King,"
still prayed the unfortunate Armstrong, and other gifts shall be yours.

"Bauld four-and-twenty sisters' sons
    Shall for thee fight though a' should flee."

But even when the luckless Johnnie had added to his other splendid offers the promise that all dwellers between Gilnockie Tower and Newcastle town should pay yearly rent for the enrichment of the royal treasury, the King's cry was still " Away, away, thou traitor strang !"   Johnnie, now knowing that his life was forfeited past redemption, resumed his usual bold demeanour.   He repudiated with scorn the charges brought against him of dishonesty and disloyalty.   All his marauding exploits, he said, had been carried on at the expense of England, and were he to live for a hundred years that country should have found him in beef and mutton, meal and malt, James's own subjects remaining unharmed. All our sympathies go with the laird of Gilnockie as he exposes the King's perfidy, and laments that in trusting to the good faith of his sovereign liege, he had committed a fatal mistake.

> " To seek het water beneath cauld ice,
>   I trow it is a great follie ;
> I have asked grace at a graceless face,
>   But there is nane for my men and me.
>
> " But had I kenn'd as I cam frae hame,
>   How thou unkind wad'st been to me,
> I would have kept the Border side,
>   In spite of a' thy peers and thee.
>
> " Wist England's king that I was ta'en,
>   O gin a blithe man he wad be !
> For aince I slew his sister's son,
>   And on his breast-bane brak a tree."

At this fateful interview the Border chief was
as luxuriously apparelled as the King of Scots,
and it is the subject, not the sovereign, who
carries the honours of true majesty throughout.

Johnnie wore a girdle about his middle,
    Embroidered over wi' burning gold,
Bespangled wi' the same metal,
    Maist beautiful was to behold—

There hung nine targets at Johnnie's hat,
    And ilk ane worth three hundred poun.

"What wants that knave a king should
have?" said James to his followers, and then
he asked the chief—

"O where got ye these targets, Johnnie,
    That blink sae brawly abune thy bree?"

Prompt and overwhelming was the response—

" I got them in the field fighting,
    Where, cruel King, thou durstna be.

" Had I my horse, and harness gude,
    And riding as I wont to be,
It sud hae been tauld this hundred year,
    The meeting of my King and me."

Johnnie's last words, on being led off to
execution, present him in an amiable light,
and are truly pathetic :—

" God be with thee, Charlie, my brither,
    Lang live thou laird of Mangertoun;
Lang mayst thou live on the Border side
    Ere thou see thy brither ride up and down.

" And God be with thee, Christy, my son,
    Where thou sitt'st on thy nurse's knee;
But an thou live this hundred year
    Thy father's better thou 'lt never be.

" Fareweel, my bonnie Gilnock ha',
    Where on Esk-side thou standest stout;
If I had lived but seven years mair,
    I wad hae gilt thee round about."

Long long did the ladies of Langholm look
for the return of the gallant band and their
chief, and loud would be their lament when
the tidings reached them that their husbands,
brothers, and lovers had been barbarously
hanged on the growing trees which over-
shadowed the scene of their fatal interview
with the Rhadamantine King.   Their dool
and sorrow, according to the balladist, were
shared by the country at large.

Johnnie murdered was at Carlinrigg,
    And all his gallant companie;
But Scotland's heart was ne'er sae wae
    To see sae monie brave men dee—

Because they saved their country dear
  Frae Englishmen; nane were sae bauld:
While Johnnie lived on the Border side,
  Nane of them durst come near his hauld.

THE OUTLAW MURRAY.

A different treatment was given by James V. to another powerful marauder, known as the Outlaw Murray, who ruled like a petty sovereign in Ettrick Forest. Commissioned by the King, James Boyd, Earl of Arran, proceeded to Newark Lee, and on finding Murray there, surrounded by five hundred brawly buskit bowmen, accosted him thus:—

  "The King of Scotland sent me here,
    And, gude outlaw, I am sent to thee;
  I wad wot of whom ye hold your lands,
    Or, man, wha may thy master be?"

  "Thir lands are *mine*," the outlaw said,
    "I ken nae King in Christendie;
  Frae Southron I this Forest wan
    When the King nor his knights were not
      to see."

Then replied Boyd, " He desires you 'll come to Edinburgh, and hold of him the Forest free," failing which, the King will seize Ettrick, make a widow of the outlaw's wife, and hang all his merry men pair by pair. Boyd, on

returning back to his sovereign, described the
defiant attitude of Murray—

> " He says yon Forest is his ain,
>   He wan it frae the Southronrie ;
> Sae as he wan't, sae will he keep it,
>   Contrair all kings in Christendie."

To raise an army with which to crush the
haughty rebel was James's prompt resolve.

> " Gae warn me Perthshire and Angus baith,
>   Fife up and down, and Lothians three,
> And graith my horse," said our noble king,
>   " For to Ettrick Forest hie will we."

Murray, having got an inkling of the
threatened royal raid, swore he would resist
it to the uttermost if he could only rely upon
getting help from kinsmen three, namely,
Halliday of Corehead, his sister's son ;
Andrew Murray of Cockpool, his cousin ; and
another relative, James Murray of Traquair.
All these yeomen, when appealed to, promised
to assist Murray in his hour of need ; and they,
well knowing that in aiding him they would
render service to themselves, as " landless
men they a' wad be " if the King got his own
way in Ettrick Forest.   Halliday, in his
return message, said, " Ay, by my troth, I'll
help my mother's brother, for gif he lose the
fair Forest," Moffatdale would soon become
too hot for his nephew.   With 5000 men

James crossed the Tweed at Caddon Ford, near Yair. About 1500 troopers, skirting their sylvan stronghold, blocked his march, making the Forest, which was usually termed " fair," wear a black aspect in the eyes of the royalists. For the purpose of preventing a sanguinary collision, Lord Hamilton suggested a friendly conference, for which advice he was rebuked by the " Laird of Buckscleuch," " a stalwart man and stern," the chief of the Scotts adding that the King would lower his dignity were he to hold converse with such a disreputable fellow as Murray.

> " The man that wons yon Forest intil
>   He lives by reife and felonrie,
> Wherefore, brayd on, my sovereign liege,
>   Wi' fire and sword we 'll follow thee,
> Or, gif your countrie lords fa' back,
>   Our Borderers sall the onset gie."

James silenced Buccleuch with one of the witty gibes he liked to indulge in when warranted, as on this occasion—

> Then out and spak the noble King,
>   And round him cast a wilie e'e,
> " Noo haud thy tongue, Sir Walter Scott,
>   Nor speak of reif nor felonrie ;
> For had every honest man his ain,
>   A richt puir clan thy ane wad be."

Acting upon Hamilton's prudent advice, James sent forward Pringle of Torsonce to arrange for a conference : the place Permanscore ; Murray, with four friends, to take part in it on one side, the sovereign, with five earls, on the other. It was some time before the Forest chief made up his mind to incur the risk which the interview involved. Consenting at length, he, accompanied by "auld Halliday and young Halliday," and the two Murrays, proceeded to Permanscore.

> When that they cam before the King.
>   They fell before him on their knee.
> " Grant mercie, mercie, noble King,
>   E'en for His sake that died on tree."

James, assuming a threatening air, told the petitioners they were but a pack of vile thieves, who did not deserve to live a day longer ; and it seemed as if he were about to act as treacherously towards them as he had done to the Gilnockie Armstrongs. The five earls supported the outlaw's petition as he tried to bargain for pardon and something more, offering tempting terms thus—

> " I 'll give thee the keys of my castell,
>   Wi' the blessing o' my gay ladye,
> Gin thou 'lt mak me sheriff of this Forest,
>   And a' my offspring after me."

Truly a liberal-minded knave, thought the
King; honest, too, in his own way; and as
for his followers, they seem brave fighting
men, who may yet render good service to the
State. James being in this mood, we marvel
not that to mercy he adds a liberality that is
right royal.

" Now name thy lands where'er they lie,
    And here I render them to thee."

" Fair Philiphaugh is mine by right,
    And Lewinshope still more shall be,
Newark, Foulshiells, and Tinnies baith,
    My bow and arrow purchased me.

" And I hae native steads to me,
    The Newark Lee and Hangingshaw.
I hae monie steads in the Forest fair,
    But them by name I dinna knaw."

We can fancy the joyous air manifested by
the old sympathetic minstrel as he thus closes
his interesting narrative—

The key of the castell he gave the King,
    Wi' the blessing o' his fair ladye;
He was made sheriff o' Ettrick Forest,
    Surely while upward grows the tree;
And if he wasna traitour to the King,
    Forfaulted he suld never be.

Wha ever heard, in onie time,
  Siccan an outlaw in his degree,
Sic favour get before a king,
  As the Outlaw Murray o' the Forest free?

JAMIE TELFER.

One day about the Martinmas-tide, Jamie Telfer of Dodhead in Teviotdale received an unexpected visit from the Captain of Bewcastle. In consequence his cattle were driven off, his house "ranschakled," so that poor Jamie's heart was sair, "the tear aye rowing in his e'e." Mercilessly exactive was the English reiver; but the sorely-plundered Scot resolved in his heart to exact reprisals by making a counter-foray across the Tweed. The narrative of the steps he took for that purpose supplies a vivid illustration of Border life in the old cattle-lifting times. During the gloaming of the doleful day that had seen his homestead harried, when "the sun wasna up, but the mune was doun," he ran twelve miles afoot to Stobs's Ha', at the gates of which he bawled aloud—

Till out bespak auld Gibby Elliot—
  " Wha 's this that brings the fray to me ? "

" It 's I, Jamie Telfer o' the fair Dodhead,
  And a harried man I think I be ;

There 's naething left at the fair Dodhead
But a waefu' wife and bairnies three."

" Gae seek your succour at Branksome
Ha'," cried the old carle, who seems to have
been a crusty piece of rough-spun, without any
silken thread of chivalry in his composition—

" Gae seek your succour where ye paid
     blackmail ;
Fy, man ! ye ne'er paid money to me."

Hurrying off to Coultercleugh, Telfer told
his wants in the same way to its occupier,
auld Jock Grieve, who, being his brother-in-
law, recognised the relationship by present-
ing Jamie with a bonnie black steed, a most
welcome gift to the footsore traveller. With
courage quite revived, he rode to the Catslack-
hill, and was lucky enough to secure the per-
sonal services of William's Wat, its laird, and
of his two stalwart sons. Branksome Hall
was the destination of the four troopers.
How well that stronghold was furnished with
fighting men, ready at a moment's warning to
take the field, is charmingly told in *The Lay
of the Last Minstrel*—

Nine-and-twenty knights of fame
     Hung their shields in Branksome Hall ;
Nine-and-twenty squires of name
     Brought them their steeds to bower from
          stall ;

Nine-and-twenty yeomen tall,
Waited, duteous, on them all :
They were all knights of mettle true,
Kinsmen to the bold Buccleuch.

Ten of them were sheathed in steel,
With belted sword, and spur on heel ;
They quitted not their harness bright,
Neither by day, nor yet by night :
      They lay down to rest
      With corset laced,
Pillow'd on buckler cold and hard ;
      They carved at the meal
      With gloves of steel,
And they drank the red wine through the
      helmet barr'd.

Ten squires, ten yeomen, mail-clad men,
Waited the beck of the warders ten :
Thirty steeds, both fleet and wight,
Stood saddled in stable day and night,
Barbed with frontlet of steel, I trow,
And with Jedwood-axe at saddle-bow :
A hundred more fed free in stall :—
Such was the custom of Branksome Hall.

Not in vain did Jamie Telfer appeal for help
to the powerful chief who had such a follow-
ing at his command. Buccleuch selecting, I
fancy, a portion of his standing force, took
means for supplementing it by causing the

water to be warned—a summons in the fiery
cross style, to be sent to all the Scotts of the
countryside—

> " Gar warn the water braid and wide,
>   Gar warn it sune and hastilie :
> They that winna ride for Telfer's kye,
>   Let them never look in the face o' me.

> " Warn Wat o' Harden, and his sons,
>   Wi' them will Borthwick water ride ;
> Warn Gaudilands, and Allanhaugh,
>   And Gilmanscleuch, and Commonside.

> " Ride by the gate at Priesthaughswire,
>   And warn the Currors o' The Lee ;
> As ye come doun the Hermitage Slack,
>   Warn doughtie Willie o' Gorinberry."

A goodly muster of armed men responded
to this arousing appeal, and, accompanied by
Telfer and his kinsfolk, off they set on the
trail of the Bewcastle trooper.

> The Scotts they rode, the Scotts they ran,
>   Sae starklie and sae steadilie ;
> And aye the ower-word o' the thrang
>   Was " Rise for Branksome readilie."

Soon they descried the stolen cattle " driving
richt fast on Frostylee."   Buccleuch's eldest
son Willie, who commanded the party, hailed

the Captain of Bewcastle as soon as they came
within speaking distance—

> "O will ye let Telfer's kye gae back?
>   Or will ye do aught for regard o' me?"

Or will ye dare the dree refusal? The bold
Englishman let his challenger know at once
that he meant to keep the hirsel—

> " I winna' let the kye gae back,
>   Neither for thy love nor for thy fear ;
> But I will drive James Telfer's kye,
>   In spite of every Scott that 's here."

> " Set on them, lads," quo' Willie then,
>   " Fye, lads, set on them cruellie ;
> For ere they win to Ritterford,
>   Monie a toom saddle there shall be."

A tremendous conflict ensued, during which
the gallant heir of Branksome fell, death-
stricken, on seeing which Wat Harden " grat
for very rage." Then brushing away his tears—

> " Revenge ! revenge !" Auld Wat gan cry,
>   " Fye, lads, lay on them cruellie ;
> We 'll ne'er see Teviotdale again
>   Unless Willie's death revenged shall be."

> O monie a horse ran maisterless,
>   The splintered lances flew on hie ;
> But ere they wan to the Kershope ford,
>   The Scotts had gotten the victorie.

During the strife, the English Captain who
originated all these troubles was crippled for
life and carried away prisoner; and the
victors, at the suggestion of one "Watty wi'
the Wudspurs," completed their retaliatory
exploits by making a fell descent upon the
enemy's hold.

> When they cam to the Stanegirthside
>   They dang wi' trees and burst the door;
> They loosed out a' the Captain's kye,
>   And set them forth our lads before.

They were boldly challenged by one of the
owner's kinswomen, "an auld wife ayont the
fire"—the reader will recollect how the
author of *Rob Roy* puts these words in the
mouth of the famous cateran when reminding
Bailie Nicol Jarvie of the ancient carline who
"made some mixture o' their bludes." Heed-
less of all remonstrance, Wudspurs Watty
caused the cattle to be turned out, and driven,
along with the re-captured herd, to Telfer's
house.

> When they cam to the fair Dodhead,
>   They were a welcome sicht to see,
> For instead of his ain ten milk-kye,
>   Jamie Telfer has gotten thirty and three.

So far the raid that looked so unpromising
at first, proved marvellously successful; but

the rejoicings which it prompted were kept in check by a feeling of sympathy on the part of the troopers for the family at Branksome Hall, because of their sore bereavement. At the burial of Willie Scott

I wat was monie a weeping e'e ;

and be sure Jamie Telfer, who grat for the loss of world's gear, would " let the tears dounfa' " when he saw the remains of his chieftain's young son laid in the dust.

KINMOUNT WILLIE.

William Armstrong of Kinmount, a renowned mosstrooper, having been taken prisoner by Lord Scroop, the English warden, in defiance of a truce existing between the kingdoms, the Lord of Buccleuch, who had the charge of Liddesdale, requested that he should be set at liberty. No answer having been received, the Scottish warden, with 200 of his vassals, resolved to secure Armstrong's freedom by force. Mark the noble indignation of the " bauld keeper " when tidings were brought to him of what had occurred.

" Oh, is my basnet a widow's curch,
　　Or my lance a wand o' the willow tree ;
　Or my arm a lady's lilye hand,
　　That an English lord should lightly me."

" And have they ta'en him, Kinmount Willie,
  Against the truce of Border tide,
And forgotten that the Bauld Buccleuch
  Is keeper here on the Scottish side?

" O were there war between the lands,
  As weel I wot that there is nane,
I would slight Carlisle Castle high,
  Though it were builded of marble stane.

" I would set that castle in a low,
  And sloken it wi' English blood ;
There 's never a man in Cumberland
  Should ken where Carlisle Castle stood.

" But since nae war 's between the lands,
  And there is peace, and peace should be,
I 'll neither harm English lad nor lass,
  And yet the Kinmount freed shall be."

Dividing his men into companies, the last
was arranged five and five, like " a mason
gang," carrying the ladders that were requisite
for their daring enterprise. In crossing the
Debatable Land, who should they meet with
but the " fause Sakelde," who greeted them
thus—

" Where are ye gaun, ye mason lads,
  Wi' a' your ladders lang and hie ? "

Prompt and humorous was the answer—

" We gang to herrie a corbie's nest
  That wons not far frae Woodhouslee."

Though the river Eden was in high flood, they crossed it safely at Staneshaw-bank, and amid a dreadful storm of " wind and weet, of fire and sleet " they reached the fortress-prison of the freebooter. By creeping stealthily on hands and knees they got near enough to place the ladders. Buccleuch, true to his *nom de guerre*, boldly mounted first, and seizing the sentinel, flung him down upon the leads. Secrecy and silence were now no longer necessary; and, by creating a prodigious racket, the garrison would be led to believe that their foes were legion. Accordingly trumpets were blown, the slogan was sounded. and all the tumultuous clangour of a warlike assault was indulged in. The effect is thus described—

> They thought King James and a' his men
>   Had won the house wi' bow and spear,
> Though 'twas but twenty Scots and ten
>   That put a thousand in sic a steer.

Cutting a hole through a sheet of lead in the roof, they thus reached the castle hall; and then

> Wi' coulters and wi' fore-hammers,
>   We garr'd the bars gang merrilie,
> Until we cam to the inner prison,
>   Where Willie o' Kinmount he did lie.

The prisoner, little dreaming of the good
fortune that awaited him, was then addressed
by some one on the outside, who asked if he
were asleep or awake. There is a true touch
of nature in the reply—

" Oh, I sleep saft, and I wake aft,
    It's lang since sleeping was fleyed frae
        me ;
Gie my service back to my wife and bairns,
    And a' guid fellows that speir for me."

But a bold brother reiver, named Red Rowan,
the starkest man in Teviotdale, soon got in
beside the captive, and announced the glad
news that he would be able in a trice to bear
his own message to the guidwife of Kin-
mount. Willie, delighted, took formal and
witty farewell of his keeper thus—

" Fareweel, fareweel, my gude Lord Scroop,
    My gude Lord Scroop, fareweel," he cried;
" I 'll pay ye for my lodging mail
    When first we meet on the Border side."

But heavily ironed was Kinmount Willie ;
his deliverers had no time to file off his chains,
so he had to mount horseback fashion on
the stalwart trooper of Teviotdale. While

being thus awkwardly carried off, the wit of
the liberated yeoman flashed forth anew—

Then shoulder-high, with shout and cry,
  We bore him down the ladder lang,
At every stride Red Rowan made
  I wat the Kinmount's airns played clang.

" O mony a time," quo' Kinmount Willie,
  " I 've pricket a horse baith wild and wud,
But a rougher beast than Red Rowan
  I ween my legs have ne'er bestrode."

" And mony a time," quo' Kinmount Willie,
  " I 've pricked a horse out owre the furs,
But since the day I backed a steed,
  I never wore sic cumbrous spurs."

Off, however, they hied, with triumphant
success, and as they returned the river was still
foaming and raging like a troubled sea.   But
they had nothing else for it but to dash into
the dangerous deluge, for Carlisle was now
up in alarm, and Lord Scroop, with a thousand
men, was in full cry at their heels.

Buccleuch has turned to Eden water,
  Even where it flowed from bank to brim,
And he has plunged in wi' a' his men,
  And safely swam them thro' the stream.

He turned him on the other side,
  And at Lord Scroop his glove flung he;
" If ye like na my visit to merry England,
  In fair Scotland come visit me."

All sore astonished stood Lord Scroop,
  He stood as still as rock o' stane,
He scarcely daured to trew his eyes,
  When through the water they had gane.

" He is either himsel' a devil frae hell,
  Or else his mother a witch maun be;
I wadna hae ridden that wan water
  For a' the gowd in Christendie."

THE HARPER OF LOCHMABEN.

The hero of our next and closing Border
tale is a veritable harper, who lived in the
venerable burgh of Lochmaben.   Evidently
the ballad is not his own composition, as in it
he is called rather contemptuously the " silly
blind harper;" but if somewhat weakly in
body, he was active in mind, artful as a fox,
while his professional accomplishments were,
as we shall see, so wonderful, that he must
have been very little inferior to the famous
Glenkindie,

  " Who could harp a fish out o' saut water,
    And water out o' a stane."

Well, this silly blind harper of Lochmaben town was a genuine Borderer, as well as a first-rate musician, considering that cattle, horse, gear, or goods of any kind reived from Southern loons was no robbery. The warden of the English march had a magnificent horse named Wanton Brown; and, with the view of acquiring this coveted animal, the harper has a confidential crack, or council of war, with his guidwife. His scheme being thus duly matured, he proceeds to Carlisle on the back of an old grey mare which has a foal in the stable, the crafty old minstrel confidently calculating that should the mare be let loose at his journey's end, she would hurry home to Lochmaben, drawn thither by maternal fondness for her young.

The Lord Warden was drinking the bluid-red wine with other nobles, in the "merrie citie," when the harper's marvellous music was heard sounding at the gate. He was straightway invited in; but he bargained first for stabling to his mare, and so the Warden ordered his groom to tie up the old beast beside his Wanton Brown — the very thing that the old minstrel desired. Good luck has favoured the beginning of the plot, and his instrument must carry it on with success; and so he draws bewitching strains from its strings—

Aye he harpit, and aye he carpit,
  Till a' the lordlings footed the floor ;
But as the music was sae sweet,
  The groom had na mind o' the stable door.

And aye he harpit, and aye he carpit,
  Till all the nobles were fast asleep ;
Then quickly he took off his shoon,
  And softly doun the stairs did creep.

He's off to the stable, and you will perhaps say
has thrown himself astride of Wanton Brown,
and is away in triumph to the North.   Not so.
That course would have been full of danger.
Fleet-footed though the English nag was, and
asleep though the nobles were, other swift
steeds were stabled in Carlisle, and watchful
sentinels hovered round about, and the silly
auld harper might have had to rue the day
when he went across the Border.   Not by an
open high-handed act of appropriation did he
try to acquire the precious animal, but by a
safe and ingenious device.

  He took a cowt halter frae his hose.
    And o' his purpose he didna fail ;
  He slipt it over the Wanton's nose,
    And tied it to his grey meare's tail.

  He turned them loose at the castle gate,
    Ower muir, and moss, and ilka dale ;

And she never let the Wanton bait,
    But kept him galloping hame to her foal.

The grey meare was richt sure o' fit,
    And didna fail to find the way;
For she was at Lochmaben yett
    Fu' lang three hours ere it was day.

What follows is so rich and racy that a
single verse must not be omitted.

When the meare cam to the harper's door,
    There she gaed mony a nicher and sneer;
" Rise up," quo' the wife, " thou lazy lass,
    Let in thy master and his meare."

Then up she rose, put on her clothes,
    And keekit through at the lock-hole,
" Ah ! by my sooth," the lassie cried,
    " Our meare has gotten a braw broun
        foal !"

" Come, haud thy tongue, thou silly wench,
    The moon 's but glancin' in your e'e.
I 'd wad my hail fee 'gainst a groat
    He 's bigger than ever our foal will be."

Now all the while, in Merry Carlisle,
    The harper harpit to hie and law,
And the fiend dought they do but listen
        him to
    Until that the day began to daw.

But in the morn, at fair day light,
  When they had ended a' their cheer,
Behold the Wanton Brown was gane,
  And eke the poor blin' harper's meare.

" Alace, alace !" says the silly blin' harper,
  " Alace, alace, that I cam here !
In Scotland I 've tint a braw cowt foal,
  In England they 've stown my gude grey
    meare."

" Come, cease thy allasing, thou silly harper,
  And again o' thy harpin' let us hear,
And weel paid shall thy cowt foal be,
  And thou shalt have a far better meare."

And aye he harpit, and aye he carpit,
  Sae sweet were the harpin's he let them
    hear ;
He was paid for the foal he had never lost,
  And three times ower for the gude grey
    meare.

PART THIRD.

TRAGICAL.

LAMMIKIN.

THAN Lammikin no more cruel monster appears in the minstrelsy of Scotland. "As gude a mason as ever hewed a stane," his goodness extended only to his handicraft.

> He biggit Lord Weire's castle,
> But payment gat he nane,

and because his account remained undis-charged, and his noble employer would come to no terms with him, he resolved to cancel the debt by destroying the fabric.

> " Sin ye winna gie me my wages, Lord.
> Sin ye winna gie me my hire.
> This gude castle sae stately built.
> I shall gar rock wi' fire."

We are led to infer that Lord Weire, instead
of trying to mollify the savage craftsman when
appealed to for the last time, treated both
claim and claimant with contempt. Yet, as if
infatuated, he prepared straightway to "seek
his pleasure in the woods." On intimating this
intention to his wedded partner, she prayed
him to give it up:

"O byde at hame, my gude Lord Weire,
  I weird ye byde at hame;
Gang nae to this day's hunting,
  To leave me a' alane.

"Yae nicht, yae nicht I dreamed this bower
  O' red, red blude was fu',
Gin ye gang to this black hunting,
  I sall hae cause to rue."

With characteristic temerity Lord Weire
threw ridicule on his wife's dream, affirmed
she had no reason to fear;

And syne he kindly kissed her cheek,
  And syne the starting tear.

Then, taking his retainers with him, he rode
off gaily to "the gude green wood" on his
sporting enterprise. Actuated by a foreboding
of immediate danger, the lady withdrew
"to her painted bower," first causing all the
windows and doors of the building to be

fastened inside. But her precautions were of little avail, as the man whom she had reason to dread had an emissary in the castle bribed over to work his will.

> They steekit doors, they steekit yetts,
>   Close to the cheek and chin ;
> They steekit them a' but a wee wicket,
>   And Lammikin crap in.

Between him and his treacherous accomplice a whispered dialogue ensued, which is rendered in a highly dramatic form—

> " Where are the lads o' this castle ? "
>   Says the Lammikin ;
> " They 're a' wi' Lord Weire hunting,"
>   The false nourice did sing.

> " Where are the lasses o' this castle ? "
>   Says the Lammikin ;
> " They 're a' oot at the washing,"
>   The false nourice did sing.

> " But, where 's the lady o' this house ? "
>   Says the Lammikin ;
> " She is in her bower, sewing,"
>   The false nourice did sing.

> " Is this the bairn o' this house ? "
>   Says the Lammikin ;
> " The only bairn Lord Weire auchts."
>   The false nourice did sing.

Surely, exclaims the gentle reader, Lammikin, cruel though he is, will provide for the safety of this innocent babe and its mother before he applies the torch of ruin to their domestic sanctuary! Alas, no! The sight of the prattling infant did not soften his heart; it rendered it, on the contrary, increasingly implacable, and gave his vengeful aims a more fiendish bent. He would discharge the bond of debt, not by fire, but by blood!

> Lammikin nipped the bonnie babe,
> While loud the false nourice sings;
> Lammikin nipped the bonnie babe,
> Till high the red blude springs.

Loud above the nurse's lullaby rose the screams of her charge, piercing the ear of its mother as she sat in her lonely turret above. Then followed another colloquy; this time between Lady Weire and her treacherous servitor—

> "Still my bairn, nourice,
> O still him if ye can!"
> "He will not still, madam,
> For a' his father's lan'."

> "O gentle nourice, still my bairn,
> O still him wi' the keys."
> "He will not still, my lady,
> Let me do what I please."

Other soothing devices were suggested by the distracted matron, with no better success. Acting under the prompting of Lammikin, the nurse at length assured her mistress that if she wished the child pacified she must come down and undertake the task herself. Unconsciously placing herself in the power of the ruthless mason, she broke up her protecting barricade and began to descend the stair. With a stage effect that might awaken the envy of a modern melo-dramatist, the old minstrel author of the ballad brings on the *dénouement*—

> The first step she steppit,
>   She steppit on a stane ;
> The next step she steppit,
>   She met the Lammikin.

Gory, gory were his hands, and the glare of his eyes spoke murder—

> And when she saw the red, red blude,
>   A loud skreitch skreitched she,
> " O monster, monster, spare my child,
>   Who never skaithed thee !

> " O spare, if in your bluidy breist
>   Abides not heart o' stane,
> O spare, and ye sall hae o' gowd,
>   What ye can carry hame."

" I care na for your gowd," he said,
  " I care na for your fee ;
I hae been wrangit by your lord,
  Black vengeance ye sall dree."

The hideous villain dilated with a grim
delight on the utter defencelessness of his
destined victim : her lord away in the distant
woods, that were ringing merrily with the
notes of his bugle-horn ; and not a soul near
by to stand between her and death. At this
awful moment a word of remonstrance is ad-
dressed by the doomed Lady Weire to the
treacherous nurse, which draws from the latter
the insolent reply—

" I wanted for nae meat, ladie,
  I wanted for nae fee,
But I wanted for a hantle
  A fair lady could gie."

Then Lammikin drew his red, red sword,
  And sharpit it on a stane,
And through and through this fair lady
  The cauld, cauld steel has gane.

" Haud awa hame !" Yet one could almost
wish Lord Weire to " bide awa" for ever-
more, rather than return to his bower to
realise the fulfilment of his murdered lady's
dream. Arrived at the postern gate, " He

thocht he saw his sweet bairn's blude sprinkled
on a stane." His apprehension of evil was
deepened by the rings of his fingers bursting
ominously in twain, and causing him to sigh,
" I wish a' may be weel wi' my lady at hame."

> But mair he looked, and dule saw he
>   On the door at the trance,
> Spots o' his dear lady's blude
>   Shining like a lance.

" Horror on horror's head accumulates," as
he hurries through the chambers of the
castle.

> " There 's blude in my nurserie,
>   There 's blude in my ha',
> There 's blude in my fair lady's bower,
>   An' that 's warst o' a'."

Rarely anywhere do we find so much
subject-matter narrated, or rather suggested, in
a single verse, as in the four lines that follow ;
and they are rendered all the more remarkable
by the cheerful accessory which, Hogarth-
like, the painter-poet introduces into his pic-
ture, with the view of giving its ghastliness a
deeper shade—

> O sweet, sweet sang the birdie,
>   Upon the bough sae hie,
> But little cared false nourice for that,
>   For it was her gallows-tree.

Nor did the principal culprit escape. After finishing his bloody work, he hastened away from the scene to seek for shelter, knowing well that Lord Weire's men would follow on his trail in full cry. Not till they had rode all the country round did they find the wretched man. Before being led to execution, he was subjected to torture, in accordance with the custom of the times—

> They carried him a' airts o' wind,
> And meikle pain had he,
> At last before Lord Weire's gate,
> They hanged him on a tree.

GIL. MORICE.

The chief scenes of our next ballad are laid in a forest green. Under its leafy canopy is perceived a beautiful youth, the son of an earl, " whose fame had waxéd wide," not because of his comeliness, but because " of a lady gay, who lived on Carron-side," with whom public rumour had associated his name in an amorous intrigue. He is heard expressing a wish which gives colour to the calumny, that he could get some bonnie boy " to win baith hose and shoon " by bearing a message to " Lord Barnard's ha', bidding his lady come." Need I say that the earl's son is Gil Morice. the pride of

the old minstrels, and the prototype of Norval.
the hero of Home's renowned tragedy of
Douglas. As ill-luck would have it, his page,
Willie, stood near, and, on being asked to
undertake this delicate piece of service, he
replied—

> " O no, O no, my maister dear,
> I daurna for my life,
> I 'll no gae to the bauld baron,
> For to tryst furth his wife."

Gil Morice, however, will not be gainsayed.
Altering his tone, he tells the boy that he
must go, or suffer death as the penalty of
refusal ; and, becoming more explicit, he
says—

> " Gae bid her tak this gay mantle,
> It 's a' gowd but the hem ;
> Bid her come to the gude green wode.
> And bring nane but her lane ;

> " And there it is a silken sark,
> Her ain hand sewed the sleeve,
> And bid her come to Gil Morice,
> Speir nae bauld baron's leave."

No wonder that Willie entered upon his task
with reluctance, so improper and dangerous
did it seem. His master was a perfect Adonis,

a modern minstrel, true to tradition, describ-
ing him thus—

> His hair was like the threads of gold
> Drawn frae Minerva's loom;
> His lips like roses dripping dew;
> His breath was a' perfume.

This is the lovely swain who wishes to hold
secret tryst with a dainty married lady, and
sends her male apparel to facilitate the inter-
view, and render it a degree less perilous. Off
goes Willie, muttering ominous words to the
effect that, as his master would take no warn-
ing, he would have cause to rue the issue of
his black errand to Lord Barnard's castle. As
if to provoke the fulfilment of his own predic-
tion, the page, instead of proceeding cau-
tiously and stealthily, hurried past the porter
at the gate into the very presence of Lord and
Lady Barnard, and there proclaimed the pur-
port of his journey. Worse still, the malevolent
boy, producing " the gay mantle and silken
sark " in proof of his veracity, quoted the very
words that had been used respecting them by
Gil Morice. Thereupon

> The lady stampit wi' her fit,
> And winkit wi' her e'e;
> But a' that she could say or dae.
> Forbidden he wadna be.

Neither would the dour little imp follow the delusive lead of the distracted matron when she suggested that the message must have been intended for her bower-woman. His retort was witheringly conclusive—

> " I brocht it to Lord Barnard's lady ;
>   I trow that ye be she."

Coming to the rescue, " the wylie nurse, the bairn upon her knee," exclaimed—

> " If this be come frae Gil Morice,
>   It 's dear welcome to me."

But the implacable Willie, not to be foiled by this artful manœuvre, declares that the nurse is telling a pack of lies, and persistently repeats that the message he bears is to none other than Lady Barnard. Fell jealousy was meanwhile burning in the breast of the Caledonian Othello, and, losing all self-control, he behaves like one demented—

> Up and rose the bauld Baron,
>   And an angry man was he ;
> He took the table wi' his fit,
>   And kepped it wi' his knee,
> Till siller cup and mazer dish
>   In flinders they did flee.

Cooling down a little, he says—

> " Gae bring a robe o' your cleidin'
>   That hangs upon the pin,
> And I 'll away to the gude green wood,
>   And crack wi' your leman."

Bauld Lord Barnard masquerading in feminine attire! An awkward Amazon he must have appeared—much more so than the Jacobite Prince, when, disguised as a woman in Skye, his long strides almost betrayed him into the hands of the Royalists. Bonnie Charlie was fleeing for bare life; the wrathful Baron of our tale was hurrying forward on bloody errand bent, despite the tearful entreaty of his wife.[1]

[1] The views here indicated as to Lord Barnard assuming feminine apparel receive support from some verses in an old ballad entitled "Child Noryce," published by Motherwell, and which he looks upon as the most ancient composition on the subject. Lord Barnard, it is stated,

> Dressed himself in the Holland smocks,
>   And garments that was gay ;
> And he is away to the merry green wood
>   To speak to Child Nory.

> Child Noryce sits on yonder tree,
>   He whistles and he sings,
> " O wae be to me," says Child Noryce,
>   " Yonder my mother comes."

> Child Noryce he came off the tree,
>   His mother to take off the horse ;
> " Och alas, alas," says Child Noryce,
>   " My mother was ne'er so gross."

" O bide at hame now, Lord Barnard,
I wad ye bide at hame ;
Ne'er wyte a man for violence
That ne'er wat you wi' nane."

In the next verse a secret is revealed, which
the minstrel author had hitherto, with true
artistic skill, kept to himself. Against the
youthful loiterer in the grove no charge of
guilty love could with justice be brought.
The natural son of Lady Barnard, he cherished
for her the filial affection that was her due ;
and here we find him waiting longingly to be
clasped again in her fond embrace.

Gil Morice sat in gude green wood,
He whistled and he sang ;
" O, what means a' thir folk coming ;
My mother tarries lang."

When the baron reached the place of ren-
dezvous he found the object of his search
" kaiming his yellow hair"—that is to say,
putting " the threads of gold " with which
his head was dowered into seemly order in

" O *wae* be to me" is doubtless a copyist's mistake for
" O *joy* be to me." Lady Barnard's son had no occasion
to cry " Alas, alas," till he found out the real sex, and
guessed the murderous purpose of his visitor. " Child
Noryce," however, is little better than doggerel. No men-
tion is made, in the ballad of our study, of the Baron going
on horseback to meet with the object of his jealousy.

view of Lady Barnard's expected visit. If at
first the robe worn by his masculine visitor
deluded him into the belief that his mother
was drawing near, undisguised, in her own
feminine attire, he must soon have been un-
deceived by the words with which he was
saluted. and the roughness of the voice which
uttered them—

> " Nae wonder, nae wonder, Gil Morice,
>   My lady lo'ed thee weel ;
> The fairest pairt of my bodie
>   Is blacker than thy heel.

> " Yet ne'ertheless now, Gil Morice,
>   For a' thy great beautie,
> Ye 'll rue the day ye e'er was born,—
>   That head shall gae wi' me."

This, alas ! was no idle threat. The
moment after its emission the head of the
winsome youth, with its " storm of golden
hair," and the body from which it had been
ruthlessly severed by the brand of the bauld
Baron, lay, ah how gory ! " amang the leaves
sae green." Not yet sated, the remorseless
lord made arrangements for giving his wife a
horrible surprise. So affecting are the closing
verses that no one, I fancy, can read them
without emotion.

And he has ta'en Gil Morice head,
  And set it on a spear ;
The meanest man in a' that train
  Has gotten the head to bear.

The lady looked ower the castle wa',
  Beheld baith dale and doun,
And there she saw Gil Morice head
  Come trailing to the toun.

Says he, " Dost thou know Gil Morice
    head ?
  If that thou dost it see ;
Then lap it saft, and kiss it aft,
  For thou lo'est him better than me."

But when she saw Gil Morice head,
  She never spak words but three ;
" I never bore nae child but one,
  And ye 've slain him cruellie."

JOHNNIE O' BREADISLEE.

The green wood shaw, as we have already
seen, is frequently made the theatre of the
incidents out of which the old minstrels wove
their ballad dramas. Robin Hood himself
did not love the tree-covered glade more than
they, though I doubt not they often sighed as
they sang of the affecting tragedies, such as
the one just considered, that were played
out under the shade of the forest bowers.

Another of them had for locality a vast deer
forest that long stretched below the romantic
Pass of Dalveen in Durisdeer, Dumfriesshire.
Thither, on "a May morning," went Johnnie
o' Breadislee, taking with him "his gude bend
bow" and well-filled quiver, not forgetting a
leash of "gude grey dogs;" his object being
to bring home a stag or two, though he should
risk his life in the unlawful enterprise, and
despite, too, of his mother's entreaty, "O
Johnnie, for my benison, to the greenwood
dinna gang." Soon a dun deer "sleeping
aneath a bush o' broom," pierced by an
arrow from his bow, rolled dead at his feet.
Forthwith, as if Johnnie and his pack had been
fasting for days, they feasted ravenously on
their prey.

> They ate sae much o' the venison,
>   And drank sae much o' the blude,
> That Johnnie and his gude greyhounds
>   Fell asleep as they had been dead.

"A silly auld carle," seeing what had
occurred, set off to Hislinton, where dwelt
the seven keepers of the forest, and played
to them the part of a common informer.

> "As I cam doon by Merriemas,
>   And doon amang the scrogs,
> The bonniest child that ever I saw
>   Lay sleeping amang his dogs;

> " The shirt that was upon his back
>   Was o' the Holland fine,
> The doublet that was over that
>   Was o' the Lincome twine."

This young scapegrace who has been disporting himself in such a scandalous fashion must be none other than Johnnie of Breadislee. So the seven forest guardians concluded, and down they went for the purpose of punishing the audacious poacher; one of them, without avail, exhorting his brethren to be wary, as Johnnie's prodigious strength and courage were well known over the district. Waking up from his sleep, the youth found himself suddenly turned into a target for arrows without number, one of which wounded him in the knee. Nothing daunted, however, was Johnnie.

> He set his back against an aik,
>   His fit against a stane,
> And he has slain the seven foresters,
>   He has slain them a' but ane.

> He has broke three ribs in that ane's side,
>   But and his collar-bane,
> He's laid him twa-fauld ower his steed,
>   Bade him carry the tidings hame.

These almost superhuman feats carried with them a fearful penalty. Quite exhausted

with fatigue and loss of blood, the dying
youth, seeing no human friend within hail,
appealed to the feathered denizens of the
forest—

" O is there na a bonnie bird
    Can sing as I can say,
Can flee away to my mother's bower,
    And tell to fetch Johnnie away."

The next verse, in which his appeal is con-
tinued, is so exquisitely pathetic, and in every
way so beautiful, that it would be difficult to
find its match anywhere :

" O is there na a bird in a' this forest
    Will do as meikle for me
As dip its wing in the wan water,
    And straik it on my e'e-bree ?"

Responding to his cry for a messenger,

The starling flew to his mother's window
      stane,
    It whistled and it sang,
And aye the ower-word o' its tune
    Was " Johnnie tarries lang !"

They made a rod o' the hazel bush,
    Anither o' the slae-thorn tree ;
And monie, monie were the men
    At fetching our Johnnie.

> Then out and spak his auld mither,
> 　As fast her tears did fa,
> " Ye wadna be warned, my son Johnnie
> 　Frae the hunting to bide awa.
>
> " Aft hae I broucht to Breadislee,
> 　The less gear and the mair,
> But I ne'er broucht to Breadislee
> 　What grieved my heart sae sair."

In accordance, seemingly, with old burial customs, the bow of the huntsman was broken, and his hounds were killed and buried with him.

> Now Johnnie's gude bend bow is broke.
> 　And his grey dogs are slain,
> And his body lies in Durisdeer,
> 　And his hunting it is dune.

THE WOOD O' WARSLIN.

In this tragedy the chief actors are boys —two brothers, Willie and John, who, playing truant from school, went to have a wrestling match in an adjoining wood. Whilst thus engaged John was thrown, and, as he lay prostrate, a knife, falling accidentally from the ponch of Willie, " gied him a deidly wound." Thinking that the stab would not prove fatal, the dying youth prayed his brother to bear

him on his back to a stream near by, and wash
the wound till it should "bleed nae mair."
Willie did as requested; the poor boy carry-
ing his dying brother, whom he loved more
than life, to the burn-side, presenting a most
affecting picture. But the water had no cura-
tive virtue. When applied to the wound the
red tide of life flowed forth anew. John, still
hopeful, presented another request to Willie—

> "O tak ye aff my Holland sark,
> And rive it gair by gair,
> And stap it in my bluidy wound,
> And it will bleed nae mair!"

This experiment having been tried without
any good results, and John growing weaker
every minute, he became conscious at length
that his end was drawing near. Deeply
pathetic are the closing verses, in which
the dying boy gives his farewell instruc-
tions, and with true brotherly feeling, even
though it be with some degree of deceit, tries
to keep Willie free from all connection with
his death—

> "O brother dear, ye 'll lift me up,
> Take me to Kirkland fair,
> And dig a grave baith wide and deep,
> And lay my body there."

" But what shall I say to our father dear,
      When he speirs for his son John ?"
" Say that ye left him at Kirkland fair,
      Learning in school alone."

" And what shall I say to your wee sister,
      When its ' Willie, O where is John ?' "
" Ye 'll say ye left him in Kirkland fair,
      The green grass growing aboon."

" And what shall I say to our mother dear,
      Gin she cry, ' Why tarries my John ?' "
" O tell her I lie in Kirkland fair,
      And that hame will I never come."

MARIE HAMILTON.

The pathetic effusion that bears this name
was supposed by Sir Walter Scott to have
been founded on incidents recorded in Knox's
History of the Reformation, to the effect that a
Frenchwoman who served in the Queen's
chamber had given birth to and murdered an
illegitimate child, for which crime she was
executed.   Darnley is introduced by the
balladist as the betrayer of the unfortunate
damsel.

The King has gane to the abbey garden,
      And pu'ed the saving tree,
To scale the babe frae Marie's heart,
      But the thing it wadna be.

No sooner was the infant born than it disappeared, to the great scandal of the Court; Mary Stuart herself, mournfully interested in what had occurred, stepping upon the scene " wi' gowd strings in her hair," and questioning the damsel : " Where is the babe that I heard greet sae sair?" Not till the young woman had been pressed over and over again by her royal mistress did she make a confession of her guilt.

> " I rowed it in my handkerchief,
> And threw it in the sea;
> I bade it sink, I bade it swim,
> It wad get nae mair o' me."

Though the Queen retorted severely, her language was fitted to suggest hope not less than fear.

> " O wae be to thee, Marie Hamilton,
> An ill deid may ye dee !
> For if ye had saved the babie's life,
> It might have honoured thee.

> " But rise, rise up, Marie Hamilton,
> Rise up, and follow me,
> For I am going to Edinburgh town,
> A gay wedding to see."

With sad misgivings the damsel accompanied Queen Mary a long weary mile to the place of

their destination. Could they be going to a
bridal party when, save their rich apparel, all
the incidents of the dolorous road suggested
to her mind shame, misery, and death?
" Slowly, slowly rase she up, and slowly put
she on." So rapid was the march of the caval-
cade, that it elicited from her the reproachful
cry—

> " Ride hooly, ride hooly now, gentlemen,
>   Ride hooly, now, wi' me,
> For never, I 'm sure, a wearier burd
>   Rade in your companie !"

> As she gaed up the Parliament Close,
>   A riding on her horse,
> There she saw mony a burgess lady
>   Sit weeping at the Cross.

Why all this display of tears? asked the
trembling bower-woman, hopeful to the last—

> " O what means a' this greeting?
>   I 'm sure it's no for me,
> For I am come to Edinburgh town
>   A gay wedding to see."

> As she gaed up the Tolbooth stairs,
>   She gaed loud laughters three ;
> But or ever she cam doun again,
>   She was condemned to dee.

Led off at once to the scaffold, the horror-
stricken and penitent lady emitted her " last
dying speech " in terms that are exquisitely
beautiful and touching In the stanza specify-
ing the Queen's Maries, ballad poetry reaches
perfection.

" O dinna weep for me, ladies !
　Ye needna weep for me :
Had I not killed my ain dear bairn,
　This death I wadna dee."

" Cast off, cast off my gown," she said,
　" But let my petticoat be ;
And tie a napkin oure my face,
　That the gallows I may na see.

" Yestreen the Queen had four Maries,
　The day she 'll hae but three ;
There was Marie Beaton, and Marie Seaton,
　And Marie Carmichael, and me.

" O aft, aft hae I dressed the Queen,
　And put gowd in her hair;
But now I 've gotten for my doom,
　The gallows-tree to share !

" O happy, happy is the maid
　That 's born o' beauty free !
It was my dimpling rosie cheeks
　That 's been the dule o' me.

" I charge ye all, ye mariners,
    When ye sail oure the faem,
That ye let na my father or mother ken,
    But that I 'm coming hame!

" Ye mariners, ye mariners,
    When ye sail oure the sea,
O let na my father or mother ken
    I hung on the gallows-tree.

" O little did my mother think,
    That day she cradled me,
What lands I was to travel oure,
    What death I was to dee!

" O little did my father think
    That day he held up me,
That I, his last and dearest hope,
    Should hang upon a tree!"

Burns was very fond of this ballad, and the striking verse that precedes the last was quoted by him in one of his letters.

THE BARON OF BRACKLEY.

An encounter between Farquharson of Invercy and Gordon of Brackley in 1666 forms the basis of a spirited metrical tale. The ballad is one of few in which a married lady acts a most unwifely part towards her leal and loving husband; and it is otherwise unique. Down Deeside came the freebooting laird of Inverey, "whistling and playing." Full of military glee, the chief was yet bent on sanguinary deeds. "Lighting at Brackley yetts" when the day was dawing, he shouted out—

" Baron o' Brackley, O are ye within,
There's sharp swords at your yetts will gar
    your blude spin."

A bold challenge, certainly : one not to be laughed at, as it was given in the name of thirty men and three, while the garrison of Brackley consisted of only two males and sundry women folks, who knew more about milking the kye, turning the kirn, or spinning at the wheel, than the use of lethal weapons. The situation was such as demanded a pacific policy on the part of Gordon ; and, bending to necessity, he was about to allow his cattle to be driven off by Inverey without resistance, when his stony-hearted spouse, Lady Peggy, who, it appears, was wishful of early widow-hood, induced him to take the field.

The lady rase up, to the window she went ;
She heard her kye lowing ower hill and ower
    bent."

Addressing her husband, who was still in bed, she said—

" Rise up, ye baron, and turn back your kye,
For the lads o' Drumwharran are driving them
    bye."

His reply was that the thing was impossible :

" Where'er I hae ae man, I wat they hae ten."

Then said the lady, with the view of ridicul-
ing his lack of valour, and appealing to his
sense of manhood—

" Rise up, my lasses ; take rokes in your hand,
And turn back the kye : I hae you at com-
    mand.
Gin I had a husband, as it seems I hae nane,
He wadna lie in his bower, see his kye ta'en."

Then up gat the baron, and cried for his
    graith,
Says, " Lady, I 'll gang, though to leave you
    I 'm laith."

Exceedingly fond of his wife, and jealous of
his honour, he resolved to face death rather
than endure reproach at her hands ; the
chivalrous bravery displayed by him contrast-
ing strongly with the mock heroism she had
paraded.

" Come, kiss me then, Peggy ; and gie me my
    spear,
I aye was for peace, though I never feared
    weir.
Come, kiss me then, Peggy ; nor think I 'm to
    blame,
I weel may gae out ; but I 'll never win hame."

Proceeding with his tale, the minstrel, who
had a liking for Gordon, which I fancy the
reader will share, declared that

When Brackley was mounted and rade ower
    the green,
He was as bold a baron as ever was seen."

But of what avail was his boldness?—

Though there cam wi' Inverey thirty and three,
There was nane wi' bonnie Brackley but his
    brother and he ;
Twa gallanter Gordons did never sword draw,
But against four-and-thirty, waes me, what is
    twa ?"

The encounter that ensued was not a fight
but a massacre. Bonnie Brackley fell dead,
butchered by the ruthless Farquharson band ;
and

Frae the head o' the Dee to the banks o' the
    Spey
The Gordons may mourn him, and ban Inverey.

The minstrel draws some dolorous notes from his harp as a tribute to the luckless chief. Then, in a style of cutting irony, he asks a passing traveller—

"O cam ye by Brackley yetts? was ye in
    there?
Saw ye his Peggy dear riving her hair?"

"Yes," was the response; but Peggy was
"making good cheer."

"The lady she feasted them, carried them
    ben,
And laughed wi' the men that her baron had
    slain."

We are then told that the newly-made widow opened her gates to the false Inverey, ate with him, drank with him, kept him till morning,

        Syne bade him be gane,
And showed him the road whare he wadna
    be ta'en.

From a second version of the tale I take its closing stanzas, which bring out in still darker relief the cruel character and shameless conduct of its beldame heroine.

As a rose bloomed the lady, and blithe as a
    bride,
As a bridegroom bauld Invereye smiled by
    her side ;
Oh, she feasted him there as she ne'er feasted
    lord,
While the blude o' her husband was moist on
    his sword !

In her chamber she kept him till morning
    grew grey ;
Through the dark woods of Brackley she
    showed him the way ;
" Yon wild hill," she said, " where the sun's
    shining on
Is the hill of Glentanner ; one kiss and be-
    gone."

Especially beautiful, both in sentiment and
expression, is the last verse of all :—

There 's grief in the cottage, there 's grief in
    the ha',
For the gude, gallant Gordon that 's dead
    and awa ;
To the bush comes the bud, an' the flower to
    the plain,
But the gude and the brave, they come never
    again.

FAUSE FOODRAGE.

The title of Fause Foodrage is amply vindicated by the part assigned to him in the tale that bears his name. In its opening verses we find King Honour, probably one of the old Pictish rulers of Scotland, at the height of human happiness, the husband of a lovely woman who had been courted by other royal suitors, but had given to him her hand and heart. Soon, however, the scene changes; a rebellion breaks out, fomented probably by his disappointed rivals; its leaders resolve to murder the king, and they " cast kevils them amang " for the purpose of deciding who should be the assassin, the lot falling upon Foodrage, the villain of the narrative. Nothing loth, he at dead midnight finds his way to the chamber of the palace in which the royal pair were laid, he having first poniarded the sentinel at the outer gates. Notice how cautiously and stealthily he creeps through apartment after apartment to the sleeping-place of royalty—

> O, four-and-twenty silver keys
> 　Hang high upon a pin;
> And aye as ae door he did unlock,
> 　He has fastened it him behin'.

Not more startled was " the gracious Duncan " when confronted with the murderous Macbeth than were King Honour and his Queen when Foodrage appeared, deadly weapon in hand, at their bedside. A pathetic appeal addressed to the assassin drew from him the reply, " O, ye my errand weel shall learn " before I leave ; and the next moment pierced to the heart by " a knife, baith lang and sharp," the unfortunate monarch breathed his last in the presence of his agonised partner. A similar fate would have been hers had not the poor lady pleaded with success that her life might be spared " till lighter she should be." It was from no " compunctious visitings " that the murderer refrained from causing her heart's blood to mingle with the purple tide that streamed over couch and floor. His hand, I fancy, was restrained by the promptings of ambition, which, quick as lightning, fired his brain. " What if the Queen should give birth to a daughter ; might I not, by betrothing her to my son, secure the sceptre for our family in a constitutional way ? " Replying to the suppliant kneeling on the blood-dyed rushes at his feet, he let her know that if she bore a female child " weel nursit it sall be," but that if she brought forth " a lad bairn," the gallows-tree would be his heritage.

A torturing travail-time awaited the hapless

lady. Cut off in her own palace from all com-
munication with her friends; her bower-door
guarded by relays of "four-and-twenty valiant
knights," lest she should steal away outside, or
in any manner stultify the aspiring scheme on
which Fause Foodrage had set his heart.
"Love," it is said, "laughs at locksmiths;"
and who shall measure the strength of a
mother's love, or limit her resources when the
babe of her bosom, even though yet unborn, is
threatened with death, and must perish unless
prompt measures are employed for its protec-
tion? The Queen seems to have had a fore-
boding that her infant would be of the male
sex. Should the presentiment prove true, it
would enter life under a doom that could
only be averted in one way. The mother
must get out of her chamber-prison, other-
wise the doleful day that would look upon
the birth of her son would see him strangled
on the gallows. How to pass the sentinels,
who kept over her strict watch and ward?
Ply them plentifully with ale and wine. This
she did; and whilst they lay wallowing,
"drunk as any wild-wood swine," she was
struggling to squeeze herself through one of
the loop-holes of the apartment.

> " O narrow, narrow is this window,
>   And big, big am I grown ;"

but, says the balladist, the maternal sufferer was enabled to emerge safely by the Virgin Mother, whose help she had invoked. Then the liberated fugitive

> Wandered up, she wandered down,
> She wandered out and in;

till, prematurely overtaken by the pains of labour, she gave birth to a child, which, in accordance with her forebodings, proved to be of the male sex. The escape of the Queen frustrated, to some extent, the designs of the rebel chief, who had meanwhile usurped her prerogatives, and, demeaning himself as king, had taken up his abode in the palace. At his instance quest was made for the missing lady, and the device of " casting kevils " was again resorted to, this time in order to secure a leader for the searching party. As a result, Wise William had this duty assigned to him. That he merited the epithet attached to his name, and was, moreover, a man of fine delicate feeling, received ample proof when he appointed his wife to officiate as his representative. It had so happened that Wise William's spouse had just before this critical period presented him with a daughter. Born under the same planetary influences, the two babies now brought upon the scene were destined, as we shall soon learn, to exercise a powerful influence on each other's fortunes. The mother of the " lass bairn " seems to have had no great difficulty in ascertaining the whereabouts of the Queen and her child. Recently the inmate of a palace, and surrounded by all the luxuries of her exalted rank, she was found lying " in the very swines' styth " with the " lad bairn " her beside. Picturesque and pitiful was the first interview between the two mothers; the Queen's Majesty falling on her knees, to the great astonishment of her subject-sister, and declaring—

> " Oot o' this I winna rise,
>   Till a boon ye grant to me,
> To change your lass for this lad bairn
>   King Honour left me wi'."

On went the quick-witted Queen to unfold the details of the ingenious scheme she had just improvised.

> " And ye maun learn my gay goss-hawk
>   Richt weel to back a steed ;
> And I will learn your turtle-doo
>   As weel to write and read.

> " And ye maun learn my gay goss-hawk
>   To wield baith bow and brand ;
> And I will learn your turtle-doo
>   To lay gowd wi' her hand.

" At kirk and market, when we meet,
    We 'll daur mak nae avoo,
But ' Dame, how does my gay goss-hawk ?'
    ' Madame, how does my doo?' "

By this device, which Wise William's wife,
with his consent, agreed to, the life of King
Honour's heir was preserved; the Queen, with
her foster-child, however, being given over to
the custody of the usurper. Many years,
twice ten or thereby, pass away before any
new incidents of note arise. When the Prince
had grown up to man's estate Wise William
took him " a-hunting for to gang," and there
was one man who, full sure, had reason to
" rue the hunting of that day." Summer was
in its prime, the radiance of the solar orb,
though powerful, scarcely penetrated the
masses of foliage with which the forest trees
were laden, but the golden glow in which
dale and down were swathed rendered the
outlying scenery uncommonly fair and sweet;
a stately castle sitting on a verdant hill-side
received its due share of sunbeam favours ; and,
pointing to it, the wise and good veteran of the
tale thus addressed his youthful companion—

" O, dinna ye see that bonnie castle,
    Wi' halls and towers sae fair ?
Gin ilka man had back his ain,
    Of it ye should be heir."

The stripling, astonished and incredulous.
asked—

> " How I should be heir of that castle,
>   In sooth I canna see ;
> For it belangs to Fause Foodrage,
>   And he is nae kin to me."

Then Wise William gave a full revelation of
his long-hoarded secret.

> " O, gin you should kill him, Fause Foodrage,
>   Ye 'd do but what is richt ;
> For I wat he killed your father dear
>   Or ever ye saw the licht.

> " And gin ye should kill him, Fause Foodrage,
>   There is no man durst you blame ;
> For he keeps your mother a prisoner,
>   And she daurna tak ye hame."

> The boy stared wild, like a gray goss-hawk,
>   Says, " What may a' this mean ?"
> " My boy. ye are King Honour's son,
>   And your mother 's our lawful Queen."

> " O, gin I be King Honour's son,
>   By Our Ladye I swear
> This nicht I will that traitor slay,
>   And free my mother dear."

And the young hero kept his word, thereby

opening up the way to a happy finish of the
tale.

He has set his bent bow to his breast,
   And leaped the castle wa',
And soon he has seized on Fause Foodrage,
   Who loud for help 'gan ca'.

' O, haud your tongue noo, Fause Foodrage,
   Frae me ye shanna flee,"
Syne pierced him through the fause, fause
     heart,
   And set his mother free.

And he has rewarded Wise William
   Wi' the best half o' his land ;
And sae has he the turtle-doo
   Wi' the troth o' his richt hand.

PART FOURTH.

AMATORY AND TRAGICAL.

SWEET WILLIE AND FAIR ANNIE.

I BEGIN this section with "Sweet Willie and Fair Annie," one of the most complete, as it certainly is one of the most affecting of the ancient ballads, and a favourable specimen of the romantic and amatory kind.

In the first scene Willie appals the damsel by announcing that his mother will not allow him to marry her, she being tocherless. As a natural consequence they part in anger.

> O, Annie she 's gane till her bower,
>   And Willie doun the den ;
> And he 's come till his mither's bower,
>   By the lei licht o' the moon ;

his object being to see if his mother is still

bent on having a richly-dowered daughter-in-law. He tells her how he has two maidens in his eye; one of them not handsome, but who could bring him a goodly marriage-portion, the other possessed of nothing save native comeliness. The dialogue which ensues brings well out the worldly wisdom and domineering character of the old lady, and the bewildering dilemma of her son when reduced to the alternative of either crushing his own heart's affections, or showing disobedience to his parent.

> " The nut-brown maid has sheep and cows,
>   And fair Annie has nane ;
> And Willie, for my benison,
>   The nut-brown maid bring hame."

> " O, I shall wed the nut-brown maid,
>   And I shall bring her hame ;
> But peace nor rests between us twa,
>   Till death sinders us again."

> " But, alas ! alas !" says sweet Willie,
>   " O fair is Annie's face ;"
> " But what 's the matter, my son Willie.
>   She has nae ither grace."

> " Alas ! alas !" says sweet Willie,
>   " But white is Annie's hand ;"
> " But what 's the matter, my son Willie,
>   She has nae a fur o' land."

Willie gives in. and agrees to wed the ill-

favoured brunette; but still he protests patheti-
cally—

> " Sheep will dee in cots, mither,
>   And owsen dee in byre :
> And what 's this warl's wealth to me,
>   An' I get na my heart's desire."

Singularly enough he sends a confidential
messenger to Annie, inviting her to his mar-
riage with her rival. What his motive for so
doing is, we are at a loss to conceive, unless
it be that he wishes, by the presence of the
beautiful Annie at the bridal, to give a practical
rebuke to his mother's sordidness, and to show
what a sacrifice he has laid on the altar of filial
duty. This idea is strengthened by the instruc-
tions he sends that she is to come, not in mourn-
ing weeds, but in her most becoming attire.

> " She mauna put on the black, the black,
>   Nor yet the dowie brown,
> But the scarlet sae red, and the kerches
>   sae white,
>   And her bonnie locks hanging down."

The slighted maid, on receiving the invita-
tion, states that she will comply with it, but,
poor heart, declares, " I had rather that the
burial mass was mine." Then there is a
sudden revulsion of feeling. She will not only
go to the marriage, but withal dress herself
so daintily, and have such a goodly equipage

as shall even throw her rich, successful, and exulting rival into the shade, and make her lover's mother half-rue the bargain that has been made. All her pecuniary means, we may suppose, are exhausted in ministering to this idea. Mark what luxurious orders she gives, and what dazzling results are produced—

> " Maidens, to my bower come,
>   And lay gowd on my hair ;
> And where ye laid ae plait before,
>   Ye 'll now lay ten times mair.
>
> " Tailors, to my bower come,
>   And mak to me a weed ;
> And smiths unto my stable come,
>   And shoe to me a steed."
>
> At every tate o' Annie's horse-mane
>   There hang a silver bell,
> And there cam' a wind out frae the
>   south
>   Which made them a' to knell.
>
> And when she cam' to Mary-kirk,
>   And sat down on the deas ;
> The light that cam' frae fair Annie
>   Enlightened a' the place.

A most imposing illustration this is of ancient finery and parade ; and similar pictures are not unfrequent in the old minstrelsy, some of which we shall see when noticing " Young Bekie," " Binnorie," and other ballads.

No wonder that the nut-brown bride was astonished when Annie, in dazzling garments, which set off her dower of personal beauty, sailed into the place of ceremony ; and that she put perplexed inquiries to some of the party, and then to the intruder herself. Whether from malice or sheer simplicity, the bride attributed Annie's complexion to the use of cosmetics ; the fair maiden's answer is overwhelmingly bitter—

> " O where got ye that water, Annie,
>   That washes you sae white ? "
> " I got it in my mother's womb,
>   Where ye 'll ne'er get the like ;
>
> " For ye 've been washed in Dunny's well,
>   And dried on Dunny's dyke,
> And a' the water in the sea
>   Will never wash ye white."

To complete the mortification of the bride, the bridegroom manifests his unaltered love for Annie by taking a rose from his bonnet, and saying while he lays it in her lap,

> " The bonniest to the bonniest fa's ;
>   Hae, wear it for my sake."

But the madness of blighted affection is busy in the poor girl's brain, and her words foreshadow the coming tragedy when she says, in mingled contempt and despair—

"Tak up and wear your rose, Willie,
  As long as it will last ;
For, like your love, its sweetness a'
  Will soon be gane and past.
" Wear ye the rose o' love, Willie,
  And I the thorn o' care ;
For the woman shall never bear a son
  That will mak my heart sae sair."

It will be observed that these fine verses contain the germ of the leading idea of the " Banks and Braes o' Doon " by Burns, and that the scene which ensues has been drawn upon by Mallet, and other modern minstrels. The wedded pair, after retiring to rest, are aroused by an apparition—the ghost of fair Annie, who thus, in woful tones, addresses her faithless lover—

" Weel brook ye o' your brown, brown bride
  Between ye and the wa',
And sae will I o' my winding-sheet,
  That suits me best o' a'.
" Weel brook ye o' your brown, brown bride
  Between ye and the stock,
And sae will I o' my black, black kist,
  That has neither key nor lock.
" Weel brook ye o' your brown, brown bride,
  And o' your bridal bed,
And sae will I o' the cauld, cauld mools
  That soon will hap my head."

What a fearful invocation !   The contrast
between the voluptuousness of the marriage-
chamber and the noisome, narrow house was
never more forcibly drawn.   Blair has nothing
bolder on the subject in his great poem, " The
Grave."   Sad Willie rose, and again, by the
" lei light o' the moon," sped to the abode of
his true love, and in good sooth saw fair Annie
" streckit there."   What follows is all so fine
that I must give it unabridged.

> Pale Willie grew; wae was his heart.
>   And sair he sighed wi' teen ;
> " Oh, Annie ! had I kent thy worth.
>   Ere it o'er late had been !
>
> " It 's I will miss your bonnie cheek,
>   And I will kiss your chin,
> And I will kiss your clay-cauld lips.
>   But I 'll ne'er kiss woman again.
>
> " And that I was in love outdone
>   Shall ne'er be said o' me ;
> For as ye 've died for me, Annie.
>   Sae will I do for thee.
>
> " The day ye deal at Annie's burial
>   The bread but and the wine,
> Before the morn at twal' o'clock
>   They 'll deal the same at mine.

ANNIE O' LOCHRYAN.

Our next story is equally fatal in its results, and its heroine, whose name is the same, also suffers from the cruelty of her lover's mother. In other respects, however, the plot is quite different, and it is developed with great dramatic power. The scenery is the beautiful Bay of Lochryan in Wigtownshire, towards whose waters she is represented as sailing in search of her lover, who has absented himself mysteriously, and whom she suspects to be labouring under the influence of some malignant magic spell. Since Lord Gregory cannot come to her, she will go to him, and if the might of woman's love can break the sorcery which binds him, he will soon be restored to liberty and her embrace. For this purpose she proceeds in a magnificent bark, whose sails are " o' the licht green silk," and " tows," or ropes, of taffety. So charming is her mien that when—twenty leagues and three from land—she meets with a " rank robber," the pirate, instead of rifling the ship and injuring its mistress, is at once ravished and awed by her beauty. He protests that she must either be the Queen herself or the Lass of Lochryan, and politely points out the castle she is in search of, " close by the salt sea strand."

> She sailed it round, and sailed it round.
>   And loud, loud cried she,
> " Now break, now break, ye fairy charms.
>   And set my true love free."

She next uses a counter-spell of a more potent
kind, though it is equally unavailing.

> She 's ta'en yer young son in her arms,
>   And to the door she 's gane,
> And lang she knocked and sair she ca'd,
>   But answer gat she nane.

In vain she knocked during the mirk midnight
hour—in vain tirled at the pin. Her lover, in
a remote part of the tower, was fast asleep;
and his mother, hearing the entreaties of the
damsel, personated him, and affected to con-
sider her an impostor :

> " Oh, open the door, Lord Gregory !
>   Oh, open and let me in,
> For the wind blaws through my yellow
>   hair,
>   And the rain draps o'er my chin."

> " Awa, awa, ye ill woman,
>   Ye 're no come here for good,
> Ye 're but some witch or vile warlock,
>   Or mermaid o' the flood."

" I am neither witch nor vile warlock,
      Nor mermaid o' the sea,
  But I am Annie o' Lochryan—
      O, open the door to me ! "

The old termagant lady, partly for the pur-
pose of tantalising the weeping suppliant, and
partly to ascertain to what extent there had
been any intercourse between her and her
son, thus proceeds, with voice still disguised—

  " Gin thou be Annie o' Lochryan,
      As I trow thou binna she,
  Now tell me some of the love-tokens
      That past between thee and me."

  " O, dinna ye mind, Lord Gregory,
      As we sat at the wine,
  We changed the rings frae our fingers,
      And I can show thee thine?

  " O, yours was gude and gude eneuch,
      But aye the best was mine,
  For yours was o' the gude red gowd,
      But mine o' the diamond fine.

  " Now open the door, Lord Gregory,
      Open the door, I pray,
  For thy young son is in my arms,
      And he'll be dead ere day."

A most touching appeal ; and when the poor
pleading lady found, as she thought, that her

lord was adder-deaf to it. it would render her indeed desperate. Some more account of the love-tokens was asked for, but she had no heart to carry on such a bootless conversation. Broken-hearted, she left the gate.

> Fair Annie turned her round about;
>   " Weel, since that it be sae,
> May never woman that has borne a son
>   Hae a heart sae fu' o' wae.
>
> " Tak doun, tak doun that mast o' gowd,
>   Set up a mast o' tree,
> It disna become a forsaken lady
>   To sail sae royally."

We now approach the climax of the narrative. Lord Gregory rises at day-dawn, telling his mother that he has had a dreadful dream—to the effect that the bonnie Lass o' Lochryan had been at his castle-gate and refused admittance, and that her lifeless form had been laid at his feet. The remorseless mother being of the Lady Macbeth cast of mind, she answered, with scornful indifference—

> " Gin it be for Annie o' Lochryan
>   That ye make a' this din,
> She stood a' last nicht at your door,
>   But I trow she wan na in."

Uttering a hasty malediction on his unnatural parent, he hurried to the shore; but

the sea, too, was pitiless, and heeded not his
frantic cries, as, rising in wrath, it dashed
the disappearing boat to pieces, and mother
and babe lay floating in the foam.

> " And hey Annie, and how Annie,
>   Dear Annie, speak to me !"
> But aye the louder he cried Annie,
>   The louder roared the sea.

Then comes the final catastrophe—

> Lord Gregory tore his yellow hair,
>   And made a heavy moan ;
> Fair Annie's corpse lay at his feet,
>   His bonnie young son was gone.

> And first he kissed her cherry cheek,
>   And syne he kissed her chin,
> And syne he kissed her rosy lips,
>   There was nae breath within.

> " O wae betide my cruel mother,
>   An ill death may she dee,
> She turned my true love frae my door,
>   Wha came sae far to me."

> Oh, he has mourned o'er fair Annie
>   Till the sun was ganging down ;
> Syne, wi' a sich, his heart it burst,
>   And his saul to heaven has flown.

Both Dr. Walcott and Burns have, we need

scarcely remind the reader, written poems based on this admirable and affecting ballad.

FINE FLOWERS I' THE VALLEY.

With the old minstrels the ballad that bears this title was a great favourite. The plot, which is simplicity itself, turns on the action of "a cruel brother," who, in revenge for a slight affront, stabs the heroine, his sister, on the day of her marriage. But though meagre in incident, the tale is poetically told and full of music, the rare double rhyme in each verse rendering it particularly effective when recited or sung. The author introduces to us three sisters, and three lords by whom they are courted, after which our attention is restricted to the fortunes of one of the ladies—Rose the Red, as I may venture to call her, in the absence of any designation given to her by the balladist. One of her sisters is clad in green, the other in yellow, the raiments of the three suggesting the melodious refrain of the ballad. "O, lady will you be my marrow?" said one of the visitors to the flower of his choice. The answer was an affirmative one, coupled with conditions—

"O, ye maun ask my father dear,"
Fine flowers i' the valley ;

" Likewise the mother that did me bear,"
  Wi' the red, green, and the yellow.

" And ye maun ask my sister Ann,"
  Fine flowers i' the valley ;
" And not forget my brother John,"
  Wi' the red, green, and the yellow.

It so happened that John, of all the members of the family, had been overlooked. So the bridegroom stated ; but deeming the unfortunate circumstance of little moment, he hurried on the preparations for his marriage.

Now when the wedding day was come,
  Fine flowers i' the valley ;
The knight would take his bonnie bride
    home,
  Wi' the red, green, and the yellow.

" Monie a lord and monie a knight " came to feast their eyes on the bright young bride ; and

There was nae man that did her see,
  But wished himself bridegroom to be.

Led down the stair by her father, " her sisters twain they kissed her there."

Her mother led her through the close,
  Fine flowers i' the valley ;
Her brother John set her on her horse,
  Wi' the red, green, and the yellow.

> " You are high, and I am low,
>   Give me a kiss before I go,"

cried the Judas-hearted caitiff.

> She was louting down to kiss him sweet.
>   Fine flowers i' the valley ;
> When wi' his knife he wounded her deep.
>   Wi' the red, green, and the yellow.

Then, I ween, Rose the Red lost her bloom. turning " pale as onie lily " ; but with rare self-control she said nothing to any one till the ruddy tide of life flowing over her gown deepened its crimson dye, and revealed the secret of her brother's treachery.

> " Ride saftly on," said the best young man.
>   Fine flowers i' the valley ;
> " I think our bride looks pale and wan,"
>   Wi' the red, green, and the yellow.

The wounded lady prayed that she might be led " over yon style " that she might " rest awhile," and then be able to proceed with the nuptial cavalcade ; but she soon afterwards became aware that the noisome grave and not the joyous bridal bed lay at the close of her journey.

> " O lead me owre into yon stair,
>   For there I 'll lie and bleed na mair."

The blood stopped flowing only when her

heart ceased to beat. Before the fatal moment came, a legacy-making scene, such as occurs in other lays of the period, is introduced, and with it our notice of this affecting ballad may be fittingly completed.

" O what will you leave to your father dear?"
    Fine flowers i' the valley ;
" The siller-shod steed that brought me here."
    Wi' the red, green, and the yellow.

" What will you leave to your mother dear?"
    Fine flowers i' the valley ;
" My velvet pall and my pearling gear,"
    Wi' the red, green, and the yellow.

" What will you leave to your sister Ann?"
    Fine flowers i' the valley ;
" My silken gown that stands its lane,"
    Wi' the red, green, and the yellow.

" What will you leave to your sister Grace?"
    Fine flowers i' the valley ;
" My bluidy shirt to wash and dress,"
    Wi' the red, green, and the yellow.

" And what will you leave to your brother
     John?"
    Fine flowers i' the valley ;
" The gates o' hell to let him in,"
    Wi' the red, green, and the yellow.

BINNORIE.

Sweet William, a dashing squire from the West, makes love to two daughters of the King. He courts them both, but eventually fixes his affections upon the younger of the two, because of her surpassing comeliness. As might be expected, Helen, the elder one, is " vexed sair," and filled with envy. What is infinitely worse, she cherishes a feeling of revenge, and remorselessly satiates it in a manner that makes the rest of the tuneful tale written on the subject sound like a long heart-rending wail drawn from the heart of the tragic muse. The two ladies go out together, at the instance of Helen, to see their father's ships come in—

> The youngest stood upon a stane,
>   Binnorie, O Binnorie ;
> The eldest came and pushed her in,
>   By the bonnie mill-dams o' Binnorie.

" O sister, sister, reach your hand !" shrieked the startled lady, " and ye shall be heir of half my land." " Not so," said Helen ; " I 'll be the heir of all your land," whether you will or no.

> " Shame fa' the hand that I should take,
>   Binnorie, O Binnorie ;
> It has twined me and my world's make,
>   By the bonnie mill-dams o' Binnorie."

The drowning girl prayed that though her sister withheld her hand, she might in pity stretch forth her glove; she even, in her desperate extremity, offered to give sweet William up to Helen, if she would only spare her life. Worthy of the foul fiend himself was the reply which these appeals elicited—

" Sink on, nor hope for hand or glove,
    Binnorie, O Binnorie ;
And sweet William shall better be my love,
    By the bonnie mill-dams o' Binnorie.

" Your cherry cheeks and your yellow hair,
    Binnorie, o' Binnorie ;
Had garred me gang maiden evermair,
    By the bonnie mill-dams o' Binnorie."

Having accomplished her fell purpose, the murderess slinks out of sight, nor is she again brought upon the stage till the curtain is about to fall ; and the further interest of the ballad centres on the lifeless body of her victim. " O father, father, draw your dam," said the miller's daughter to him, " there is a lady or milk-white swan" floating in its depths. When the mill-lade was run dry, the body of " a drowned woman " was revealed to view : and oh, so angelic was it in its beauty, and so royally apparelled, as became the daughter of the King !

Ye couldna see her yellow hair,
  Binnorie, O Binnorie ;
For gowd and pearls that were sae rare,
  By the bonnie mill-dams o' Binnorie.

Ye couldna see her middle sma',
  Binnorie, O Binnorie ;
Her gowden girdle was sae braw,
  By the bonnie mill-dams o' Binnorie.

Ye couldna see her lily feet,
  Binnorie, O Binnorie ;
Her gowden fringes were sae deep,
  By the bonnie mill-dams o' Binnorie.

Said the man of the mill and his daughter—

" Sair will they be, whae'er they be,
  The hearts that live to weep for thee."

There came a harper passing by,
  The sweet pale face he chanced to spy ;
And, when he looked that lady on,
  He sighed, and made a heavy moan.

A professional visitor to the palace, he at
once recognised the royal rank of the deceased ;
probably, too, he saw in her the lovely princess
whose charms had aforetime tasked his utmost
skill to portray.   He then proceeded to use his
instrument for another purpose—one of divina-
tion, in order to ascertain how it had come to
pass that she, who was so recently the fairest

of the fair, and the gayest of the gay, was now lying in that ghastly coffin, cold and low.

He has ta'en three locks o' her yellow hair,
    Binnorie, O Binnorie ;
And wi' them strung his harp sae rare,
    By the bonnie mill-dams o' Binnorie.

He brought the harp to her father's hall,
    Binnorie, O Binnorie ;
And there was the Court assembled all,
    By the bonnie mill-dams o' Binnorie.

He set the harp upon a stane,
    Binnorie, O Binnorie ;
And it began to play alane,
    By the bonnie mill-dams o' Binnorie.

Seemingly of themselves the chords of yellow hair gave forth melodious notes ; but a hand which no one saw was imparting vitality to the harp, and a verbal accompaniment was given in a voice familiar to all, and the last strain of which must have sounded in the ears of one of the party like a sentence of doom from the judgment-seat above—

" O yonder sits my father, the King,
    Binnorie, O Binnorie ;
And yonder sits my mother, the Queen,
    By the bonnie mill-dams o' Binnorie.

" And yonder stands my brother Hugh,
    Binnorie, O Binnorie ;

And by him, my William, sweet and true,
  By the bonnie mill-dams o' Binnorie."

But the last tune that the harp played then,
  Binnorie, O Binnorie;
Was "Wae to my sister, false Helen!"
  By the bonnie mill-dams o' Binnorie.

In this, and several other ancient ballads
we have noticed, lies the germ of modern
spiritualism.   For boldness of conception none
of them surpasses "Binnorie," and over few
of them has "the soul of music" been so
richly "shed."

HELEN OF KIRKCONNEL-LEE.

As I think of Helen Irving of Kirkconnel-
lee, at the time when her faith and troth were
pledged to Adam Fleming of Kirkpatrick, it
is of a well-born, beautiful, accomplished lady,
the pride of the whole district, whose very
presence threw a charm over the banks of
Kirtle waters, as she "gaed oot and in" to "pu'
the birks," to gather the wayside flowers, or to
pay her devotions at the parish sanctuary near
by.   Even the little lonely burial-place that
stretched around the church, must, I fancy,
have been coaxed out of its melancholy as it
caught "the glancin' o' her een."   In sooth,

the fair damsel always looked at her best and blithest when seen loitering in or near the hallowed precincts, because they were consecrated to a true love courtship carried on between her and the gallant young neighbouring squire, on whom she had promised to bestow her hand. For some reason, now unknown, Helen's friends did not care about Fleming, and they pressed her hard to discard him, and take up with young Bell, the laird of Blacket-tower, who had wooed her, but in vain. The love between the winsome lady of Kirkconnel-lee and Adam Fleming was strong and deep, rendering them one in heart and aim. Sooner would each of them have sacrificed life itself than have proved false to the vows which they had interchanged on Kirtle braes, in the hearing of the little brook, which glided quietly by their place of tryst, betraying no secrets, as less " menseful " streams have sometimes done in the minstrel's ditties. But their stealthy intercourse was known to Blacket-tower, and watched by him at times with jealous eye. On one sadly memorable occasion, during the gloaming hour, the lovers held their last interview,—" but little thought they 'twas their last." A small stone cross rises about forty yards from the present church to mark the spot ; but the finger of tradition points to an aged thorn, growing further down on the river's brink, as occupying the site of the tragedy that ensued. Once again the enamoured pair were favoured with "a draught of heavenly pleasure." When their cup of felicity is at the full, will any one who is not a fiend dare to dash it into fragments? The rival lover is within view, and, maddened by jealousy, he prepares to play the part of a demon. From an ambushed covert, on the opposite side of the stream, Bell raises his carabine, takes aim at Fleming, fires, and the next moment Helen Irving drops lifeless into her lover's arms, he himself escaping unharmed. The heroic maiden, on seeing the murderous weapon levelled at Fleming, had thrown herself before him, and received the bullet in her own bosom, thus dying in an unsuccessful but sublime endeavour to save him from death. Overwhelmed by the catastrophe, Fleming lifted up his voice in a wail of wildest agony. As interpreted by a sympathetic minstrel, it becomes a coronach of exquisite pathos, which, for depth of feeling and felicity of diction, has few parallels in all the realm of poetry out of Holy Writ.

> " I wish I were where Helen lies !
>   Night and day on me she cries ;
> O that I were where Helen lies,
>   On fair Kirkconnel-lee.

"Curst be the heart that thought the thought,
And curst the hand that fired the shot,
When in my arms burd Helen dropt,
   And died to succour me!

" O think ye na my heart was sair
When my love dropt doun and spak nae
     mair!
There did she swoon wi' meikle care,
   On fair Kirkconnel-lee."

A truce for a minute to unavailing sobs and
tears, that vengeance may have its due. The
minstrel allows Fleming to narrate how that
needful but bloody work was accomplished :—

" As I went doun the water side,
None but my foe to be my guide,
None but my foe to be my guide,
   On fair Kirkconnel-lee.

" I lighted doun, my sword did draw,
I hacked him in pieces sma',
I hacked him in pieces sma',
   For her sake that died for me.

But the sight of the murderer's mutilated
remains could bring no balm to the breast of
the man whom he had bereaved and rendered
desperate, and Fleming's lament for burd
Helen bursts forth anew—

"O Helen fair beyond compare !
I 'll weave a garland of thy hair,
Shall bind my heart for evermair,
   Until the day I dee !

"O that I were where Helen lies !
Night and day on me she cries ;
Out of my bed she bids me rise,
   Says, ' Haste, and come to me !'

"O Helen fair ! O Helen chaste !
Were I with thee I would be blest,
Where thou lies low, and takes thy rest
   On fair Kirkconnel-lee.

" I wish my grave were growing green,
A winding sheet drawn o'er my een,
And I in Helen's arms lying
   On fair Kirkconnel-lee.

" I wish I were where Helen lies !
Night and day on me she cries ;
And I am weary of the skies,
   For her sake that died for me."

The body of Helen was laid in Kirkconnel churchyard, and her distracted lover, haunted perpetually by her image, perilled his life in battle-fields abroad. Unharmed by the shafts of war, he returned home, the barb of incurable woe still festering in his heart ; and, prostrating himself on his sweetheart's grave, there breathed his last. Fleming's fervent desire—" I wish I were where Helen lies ! "—was fulfilled to the letter, and two massive slabs cover their place of rest. His tombstone bore till lately the words: " Hic jacet Adam Fleming," also some sculptured ornaments, both of which have been effaced by the hand of time. But the memory of the hapless lovers is imperishably preserved in the minstrel's verse.

This exquisite ballad has been frequently imitated by modern minstrels, with indifferent success. It inspired Lord Tennyson's noble poem. " Oriana," which, however, bears a trace of art and effort of which the old Scottish lay is totally void. Yet the following verses of the Poet Laureate echo in forcible style the heart-thrilling lament of Adam Fleming :—

> My heart is wasted with my woe,
>> Oriana.
> There is no rest for me below,
>> Oriana.

Why is the mourner inconsolable and weary of the sun ? Because his true love, like the Helen of the Dumfriesshire tale, had been shot dead before his eyes by an arrow that was

meant for him.   "Just as the steeds were to
battle going,

> "She saw me fight, she heard me call,
> When forth there stept a foeman tall,
>> Oriana,
> Atween me and the castle wall,
>> Oriana.

> "The bitter arrow went aside,
>> Oriana :
> The false, false arrow went aside,
>> Oriana :
> The damnéd arrow glanced aside,
> And pierced thy heart, my love, my bride,
>> Oriana !
> Thy heart, my life, my love, my bride,
>> Oriana !

> "I cry aloud : none hear my cries,
>> Oriana.
> Thou comest atween me and the skies,
>> Oriana.
> All night the silence seems to flow
> Beside me in my utter woe,
>> Oriana.
> A weary, weary way I go,
>> Oriana."

GLENKINDIE.

In Glenkindie we have a ballad of much originality and power, and it contains some verses of more than ordinary beauty; but as its incidents are of a revolting nature, we need not devote much time to its study. It carries us back some four hundred years, to a period when Scottish minstrelsy was in its palmiest condition; when the harper was

> Courted and caressed,
> High placed in hall a welcome guest,
> And poured to lord and lady gay
> His unpremeditated lay.

Among the balladists of his time no one occupied such a high position as he who gives his name to the tale.

> Glenkindie was ance a harper gude,
>   He harpit to the King;
> Glenkindie was ance the best harper
>   That ever harped on string.

> He could harp a fish out o' saut water,
>   Or water out o' a stane,
> Or milk out o' a maiden's breist
>   That bairn had never nane.

So charmingly did he play and sing at a banquet given by the King to his nobles, that

he was invited by his patron to entertain them
the whole night through, and was promised
for his service "a robe o' the royal pa'." A
boisterous party they must have been after
long birling at the wine, and by no means
fitting company for a gentle young damsel,
who, at the king's command, waited upon his
guests. This was none other than his own
"ae daughter." Singular though it may seem,
she was quite in her element. Delighted with
the music, she was captivated by the musician ;
and he, taking base advantage of his position,
wooed her "not wisely, but too well."

> He 's ta'en the harp intil his hand,
>   He 's harpit them a' asleep,
> Except it was the young Countess,
>   That love did waking keep.
>
> And first he has harpit a grave tune,
>   And syne he has harpit a gay ;
> And mony were the words o' love
>   That passed between them twae.

At last they separated; but the love-demented
lady invited her leman to return after the
guests had disappeared, she saying, siren-like,

> " At dawn, when cocks hae crawn,
>   And wappit their wings sae wide,
> It 's ye may come to my bower door,
>   And streek ye by my side."

She accompanied the invitation with a warning—

> "But, look you, tell na Gib, your man,
>   Of naething that ye dee ;
> For, an ye tell him, Gib, your man,
>   He 'll beguile baith you and me."

Though thus put upon his guard, what did the foolish Glenkindie do but reveal to his treacherous servant his assignation with the Countess at day-dawn, telling him at the same time—

> " Tak ye tent now, Gib, my man.
>   My bidding for to dee ;
> And, but an ye waken me in time,
>   Ye shall be hangit hie."

Gib, using the marvellous harp against its owner, harped the minstrel into a deep sleep ; and then, prompted by animal passion, stole away to the lady's bower. On tirling at the pin for admission, she put the question, " Whae is this, that opens nae, and comes in ?" " It 's I, Glenkindie, your ain true love," replied the shameless impostor, and he was allowed to enter, even though

> She kent he was nae gentle knight
>   That she had lettin in ;
> For neither when he gaed nor cam,
>   Kissed he her cheek or chin.

She interrogated her visitor too about his
hose and shoes, so suspiciously ragged and
riven, and about his yellow hair, that fell so
smoothly on his neck "late yestreen," and
was now so rudely tangled. He seems to have
overcome all her scruples by stating—

> " The hose and shoon are Gib, my man's,
>   They cam first to my hand ;
> And I 've ravelled a' my yellow hair
>   Coming against the wind."

In the next scene we see the guilty wretch
wakening up his master, and telling him he
has lain too long in bed, as all the cocks of
the north had already proclaimed the hour of
his love-tryst.   Glenkindie, never dreaming
that he had been deceived, ran to the bower
of the Countess, and, announcing his name,
craved entrance ; but she, now realising fully
for the first time how they had both been be-
trayed, resolutely refused to open the door.
She had sinned once, and she suffered so from
remorse and shame that she would not, dared
not for worlds, repeat the offence.

> " Forbid it, forbid it," says the lady,
>   " That ever sic shame betide,
> That I should first be a wild loon's lass,
>   And then a young knight's bride."

The beautiful Countess, heart-broken. lying
cold and dead, her unfortunate minstrel-lover
driven to the verge of madness by disappoint-
ment and horror, are the next incidents of
this harrowing tale. He refused, however,
to believe that her spirit had fled ; and, with
unflagging faith in the virtues of his instru-
ment, he touched its strings in the vain fancy
that she would hear its tones and live.

He 's ta'en his harp intil his hand—
   Sae mournfully it rang ;
And wae and weary 'twas to hear
   Glenkindie's dowie sang.

But cauld and dead was that lady,
   Nor heeded of his maen ;
An' he wad harp till doomesday,
   She 'll never speak again.

He 's broken his harp across his knee.
   And on the floor it flang ;
Says, " Lie ye there, for never mair
   I 'll need ye for my sang."

" Come forth, come forth now, Gib, my man.
   Till I pay you your fee ;
Come forth, come forth now, Gib, my man,
   Weel payit shall ye be."

So far it is well that poetical justice is

served out to the villain of the piece. When his ignominious death upon an extemporised gibbet is followed by the suicide of his distracted master, the sad sequel is recognised as in full keeping with the shocking incidents which led up to it.

> And he has ta'en him, Gib, his man,
>   And he has hanged him hie ;
> And he's hangit him over his ain yett,
>   As high as high could be.

> And syne he has drawn his bright broun
>   sword,
>   And thrust it through his bodie.

WILLIE'S DROWNED IN YARROW.

We now take up for study a series of pathetic ballads which have their locality in one valley—that of the Yarrow. " Rough and rude," says Professor Veitch, " was the life there for many generations ; but the blood-stains on its grassy holms have nurtured and nourished growths of sentiment so tender, so pure, so intense, as to be for ever a gain and a blessing to the human heart." [1] First let us listen to the sorrowful song of a fair

[1] *History and Poetry of the Scottish Border.*

damsel as she expresses her disappointment because the swain to whom she was betrothed had failed to meet her, according to promise, at their usual trysting-place on the Braes of Yarrow. Was ever plaint more musical, more melancholy in its expression than hers?

"Willie's rare and Willie's fair,
    And Willie's wondrous bonnie;
And Willie's hecht to marry me,
    Gin e'er he married onie.

"Yestreen I made my bed fu' braid,
    This nicht I'll make it narrow,
For a' the livelang winter nicht
    I'll lie twined of my marrow.

"Oh, gentle wind that blaweth south,
    Frae where my love repaireth,
Convey a kiss frae his dear mouth,
    And tell me how he fareth.

"O tell sweet Willie to come doun,
    And bid him no be cruel;
And tell him no to break the heart
    Of his love and only jewel.

"O tell sweet Willie to come doun,
    And hear the mavis singing,
And see the birds on ilka bush,
    And leaves around them hinging."

All the forest might be full of melody, and attractive in its garniture, even though the summer-tide had passed away; no need, however, had Willie for such allurements to the spot which was made a paradise to him by the presence of his true love, and whose pathetic canticle, could he only have heard it, would have exercised more magnetic influence over him than all the choristers of the grove. As the zephyr, when appealed to, brought no response from her absent sweetheart, she interrogated a passing wayfarer.

> " O cam you by yon water-side,
>   Pu'ed ye the rose or lily ?
> Or cam ye by yon meadow green,
>   Or saw ye my dear Willie ?"

The negative answer received by the poor lady drove her to despair; and we can conceive of her wail becoming charged with agony like that of " Mariana in the moated grange "—

> " He cometh not," she said ;
> She said, " I 'm aweary, aweary,
>   I would that I were dead !"

Actuated by a presentiment of unspeakable evil, which was too surely fulfilled,

> She sought him east, she sought him west,
>   She sought him broad and narrow,
> Syne in the cleaving of a craig
>   She found him drowned in Yarrow.

THE DOWIE DENS O' YARROW.

More doleful still than the foregoing is the tale entitled "The Dowie Dens o' Yarrow." Three lords, we are told, sat "birling at the wine," two of whom quarrelled. According to tradition founded upon facts, these were a Scott of Tushielaw and a Scott of Thirlstane, brothers-in-law, who had differed about some lands which old Tushielaw had conveyed to his daughter. The balladist, however, gives another version of the strife.

> " You took our sister to be your wife,
>   And thought her not your marrow :
> You stole her frae her father's back
>   When she was the Rose o' Yarrow."

To this provoking taunt from young Tushielaw, his relative, admitting the fact on which it was founded, simply said in reply—

> " I took your sister to be my wife,
>   And I made her my marrow ;
> I stole her frae her father's back,
>   And she's still the Rose o' Yarrow."

Yet the two men, before rising from their

revels, "set a combat them amang, to fight it
on the morrow." Then Thirlstane

> Has hame to his lady gane,
>   As he had done before, O ;
> Says " Madam, I maun keep a tryst
>   On the dowie dens o' Yarrow."
>
> " O bide at hame, my lord," she said,
>   " O bide at hame, my marrow,
> For my three brethren will slay thee
>   On the dowie dens o' Yarrow."

Say not so, said the husband fondly,

> " For what needs a' this sorrow,
> I 'll soon come back to thee again
>   From the dowie dens o' Yarrow."
>
> She kiss'd his cheek, she kaim'd his hair,
>   As she had dune before, O ;
> Gied him a brand doon by his side,
>   And he 's awa to Yarrow.

When Thirlstane reached the place of meet-
ing he found not one combatant only awaiting
him, nor yet three, but nine or ten, all bent
on shedding his blood, though, to put him off
his guard, they greeted him in friendly terms.

> " O come ye here to hawk or hound,
>   Or drink the wine sae clear, O ?
> Or come ye here to part your land
>   On the dowie dens o' Yarrow ?"

Not for any of these peaceful purposes am I here, said the bold laird of Thirlestane in effect, " but I'll fight wi' you on Yarrow."

Four has he hurt, and five has slain,
    On the bloody braes o' Yarrow,
Till a cowardly man cam' him behin',
    And pierced his body thorough.

It would seem from the next verse that his wife had sent his own brother, John Scott, to the scene, with the view of protecting her husband in case of need, and that he arrived only in time to take back a message to her from her murdered husband—

" Gae hame, gae hame, my brother John—
    What needs this dule and sorrow ?
Gae hame and tell my lady dear
    That I sleep sound on Yarrow."

But the lady, sitting eerily alone, felt that the mental strain from which she suffered was unbearable. She would herself push forward and interpose, if in time, to save her good lord from the fury of her brothers, and, at all events, ascertain personally the issue of the fight. Meeting her brother-in-law John when returning, she, as if afraid to put a direct question that would draw forth an answer confirmatory of her worst forebodings, addressed him thus :

> " I dreamed a dreary dream yestreen—
>   God keep us a' frae sorrow !
> I dreamed I pu'ed the birk sae green
>   Wi' my true love on Yarrow."

> " I 'll read your dream, my sister dear,
>   I 'll tell you a' your sorrow ;
> You pu'ed the birk wi' your true love,
>   He 's killed, he 's killed on Yarrow."

The version of the tragic tale from which I have drawn here terminates abruptly; and the following stanzas, borrowed from Motherwell's edition of it, give completeness and additional pathos to the ballad. The lady, after receiving John's woful tidings, continued her journey in the direction of the " dowie dens."

> Sometimes she rade, sometimes she gaed
>   As she had done before, O ;
> And aye between she fell in a swoon
>   Lang or she cam' to Yarrow.

> Her hair it was five quarters lang,
>   'Twas like the gowd for yellow,
> She twisted it round his milk-white hand,
>   And she 's drawn him hame frae Yarrow."

This wonderful verse, whether as regards sentiment or expression, presents the very quintessence of the old Scottish minstrel's art. The author of it must, I fancy, have occupied a very high position amongst his musical brethren.

> " Oot and spak her father dear,
>   Says, " What needs a' this sorrow ?
> For I'll get you a far better lord
>   Than ever died on Yarrow."

The disconsolate daughter replied that she could never marry again, and would go as a mourning widow to her grave.

Midway between the old laureates of the Yarrow and the modern minstrels—Logan, Wordsworth, and others, who caught a portion of their inspiration as they tuned their harps to the same mournful theme—stands William Hamilton of Bangour, born in 1704, author of the " Braes o' Yarrow." " This ballad," says Motherwell, " is the finest of many fine compositions which have made that stream as truly classic as Helicon or Meander."

> " Busk ye, busk ye, my bonnie, bonnie bride,
>   Busk ye, busk ye, my winsome marrow ;
> Busk ye, busk ye, my bonnie, bonnie bride,
>   And think nae mair on the braes o' Yarrow."

In exquisite opening strains the heroine is thus
addressed by a Tweedside admirer who has
made hurried arrangements for their marriage,
though his hand is red with the blood of the
man to whom she had given her heart. His
suit is supported by her father, brother, and
sisters ; but she looks upon it with loathing,
and annihilates it with a reply that admitted
of no further parley.

" What can my barbarous, barbarous father do,
    But with his cruel rage pursue me ;
My lover's blood is on thy spear,
    How canst thou, barbarous man, then woo
        me ?

" My happy sisters may be, may be proud ;
    With cruel and ungentle scoffing,
May bid me seek on Yarrow braes
    My lover mailed in his coffin.

" My brother Douglas may upbraid,
    And strive in threatening words to move
        me ;
My lover's blood is on thy spear,
    How canst thou ever bid me love thee ?

" Yes, yes ! prepare the bed, the bed of love,
    With bridal sheets my body cover ;
Unbar, ye bridal maids, the door,
    Let in the expected husband-lover.

But who the expected husband, husband is,
   His hands, methinks, are bathed in
      slaughter;
Ah me! what ghastly spectre 's yon
   Comes in his pale shroud bleeding after?

Pale as he is, here lay him, lay him down,
   O, lay his cold head on my pillow;
Take off, take off these bridal weeds,
   And crown my waefu' heid wi' willow.

Pale though thou art, yet best, yet best beloved,
   O, could my warmth to life restore thee;
Yet lie all night between my breasts,
   Nae youth lay ever there before ye."

Just a single verse or two from the Rev.
John Logan's well-known poem. Beautiful
and bright as Eden's bowers was Yarrow-side
to its heroine when her heart was there won
by the gentle youth who was about to become
her husband. Ah! how gloomy and doleful
did its braes appear as the scene of his
murder on the night before the day that had
been fixed for their marriage. Scarce had he
gone from her last fond embrace till his ghost
appeared to her, and the water-wraith ascending,
" thrice gave a doleful groan through Yarrow."

   " For ever now, O Yarrow stream,
     Thou art to me a stream of sorrow;

> For never on thy banks shall I
>   Behold my love, the flower of Yarrow."

" They sought him east, they sought him west," all through the forest, finding him not ; but the lady herself, with the instinct of fond affection, discovered his body in the river, and " with him now she sleeps in Yarrow."

After visiting this classical region in 1814, the Bard of Rydal Mount embodied the sentiments it awakened in a very sweet poem, from which I borrow a couple of stanzas—

> " Where was it that the famous Flower
>   Of Yarrow Vale lay bleeding ?
> His bed perchance was yon smooth mound
> On which the herd is feeding : '
> And haply from this crystal pool,
> Now peaceful as the morning,
> The Water-wraith ascended thrice —
> And gave his doleful warning.
>
> Delicious is the Lay that sings
> The haunts of happy Lovers,
> The path that leads them to the grove,
> The leafy grove that covers :
> And Pity sanctifies the Verse
> That paints, by strength of sorrow,
> The unconquerable strength of love ;
> Bear witness, rueful Yarrow !"

Commenting generally on the ancient lays of

Yarrow, Professor Veitch truly remarks : "The power of these old strains lies simply in this, that they indicate in the simplest, readiest words the realism, the power, the pathos of our primary human emotions—deepest love, saddest sorrow, unflinching courage, and noble self-sacrifice. This is what touched the heart of Scott, purified and inspired him, and made him ashamed of eighteenth century conventionalism."

THE MARCHIONESS OF DOUGLAS.

The principal characters in our next tale are the Marchioness of Douglas, whose father was the Earl of Mar; her husband, who parted from her under the influence of jealousy; and Lowry of Blackwood, a former lover, who, because she had rejected him, acted like another Iago in poisoning the mind of the Marquis against his spouse. Many verses of the ballad take the form of a wail wrung from the breast of the hapless lady. Full of dolour it is, and embodied in touching language, that renders it tearfully pathetic. Opening with the following verses, the ballad breathes throughout a similarly despairing spirit till towards the end; and when the end comes, and the Marchioness ceases her lament, the

sympathetic reader will be led to continue the
" waly, waly " of the strain :—

> " O, waly, waly up the bank,
>   And waly, waly doun the brae,
> And waly, waly by yon burn-side,
>   Where me and my love were wont to gae.

> " Hey nonnie, nonnie, but love is bonnie
>   A little while, when it is new :
> But when it 's auld it waxes cauld,
>   And fades away like the morning dew.

> " I leaned my back against an aik,
>   And thocht it was a trustie tree ;
> But first it bowed and syne it brak,
>   And sae did my fause love to me.

> " O, wherefore need I busk my heid,
>   And wherefore need I kaim my hair :
> For my gude Lord has me forsook,
>   And says he 'll never love me mair.

> " Gin I had wist before I kist
>   That love had been sae ill to win,
> I had lock't my heart wi' a key o' gowd,
>   And pinn'd it wi' a siller pin.

After contrasting the sweet memories of the
honeymoon with the bitterness of the present

hour, she proceeds to tell how when she lay
"sick and very sick," suffering the pains of
child-bearing, and "like to dee," a gentleman
friend paid her a visit, which had been repre-
sented to her Lord as of too long duration by
the treacherous Lowry. Then, overhearing
her husband speak lightly of her, as if he
credited the slanderous impeachment, she
cried out as loud as her weak condition would
allow—

" Come doun, come doun, O Jamie Douglas,
    And drink the orange wine wi' me,
And I 'll set thee on a chair of gowd,
    And dant thee kindly on my knee."

Nay, nay ! our days of conjugal delight are
over, and gone never to return. How im-
placably did Douglas express this conviction !

" When cockle-shells turn siller bells,
    When wine draps red frae every tree,
When frost and sna' will warm us a',
    Then I 'll come doun and dine wi' thee."

No sooner did the Earl of Mar hear how
cruelly his daughter had been treated than he
sent five-score soldiers to take her back to her
own land north of the Tay. Loving her hus-
band still, Lady Douglas made renewed over-
tures to him by whispering a few tender words

into the lattice of his chamber; and when he took no notice of her appeal, she entreated him, with no better success, to relent, if not on her account, for the sake of their sweet babe, newly born, who had never done his father harm. Thereupon, with the characteristic spirit of her race, she bade him adieu:

> " Fare ye well, then, Jamie Douglas!
>   I need care as little as ye for me,
> The Earl of Mar is my father dear,
>   And I soon will see my ain countrie.

> " Ye thocht that I was like yoursel',
>   And loving ilk ane I did see;
> But here I swear by the heavens dear
>   I never loved a man but thee."

A malediction on Blackwood followed:

> " Aye, and an ill death may he dee,
> Ye were the first and foremost man
>   That pairted my gude Lord frae me."

Arrived on her father's estate, she received a hearty welcome from his tenants, but " sighing and sobbing " she could not adequately express her thanks.

> Never a word she could speak to them,
>   But the buttons aff her clothes did flee.

   " The linnet is a bonnie bird,
      And aften flees far frae its nest :
   Sae a' the world may plainly see
      They 're far away that I loe best."

The father and daughter had a loving conference, during which he exhorted her to take comfort, as he would get her freed from her marriage bonds by a divorce, and provide for her a better husband. To these proposals she refused to listen ; and one day, while nursing her grief, a band of four-score soldiers, bearing the Douglas blazonry, rode up to the gates of her father's castle. She was bidden to come down by the leader of the party, and go back with him to her husband, now convinced of her innocence, and waiting, near at hand, to take her home. " Not a step shall you go," said the Earl of Mar.

   " Now haud your tongue, my father dear,
      And of your pity let me be,
   For I'll gae back to my gude Lord,
      Since his love has come back to me."

How distressing is it to find that the bright prospect thus opened up was but " the smiling of fortune beguiling," and that the luckless lady was compassed about by the shadow of death even when she rode forth for " home, sweet home," accompanied by a brilliant retinue, and apparalled like a queen.

She laughed like onie new-made bride
  When she took farewell of her father's
    bowers,
But the tear, I wat, stood in her e'e
  When she cam in sicht o' her lover's towers.

As she came by the orange gate,
  Whatever a blithe sicht she did see,
Her gude Lord coming her to meet,
  And in his hand her bairnies three.

After Douglas had embraced her tenderly he told her that Blackwood had met with his deserts on the gallows-tree. Then, in the height of his exultation, on their arrival at home, he cried :—

  " Gae fetch to me a pint of wine,[1]
    That I may drink to my ladie."

Taking the proferred chalice from his hand, she had scarcely put it to her lips when she fell lifeless—" her bonnie heart it brak in three."

THE DOUGLAS TRAGEDY.

History and tradition are rife with tragical events in which the patrician house of Douglas is mixed up. One of them originated in the

[1] With this line Burns begins one of his finest lyrics, " My Bonnie Mary."

Tower of Blackhouse, Selkirkshire, the ruins of which are still to be seen rising on the dark heather-clad heights which overlook the Douglas Burn. From this old peel Lady Margaret Douglas was carried away, under cloud of night, by her lover Lord William, to the great indignation of her father and seven brethren. The story of her abduction and its results is told in the vigorous ditty I am about to notice. Mounting the damsel on a milk-white steed, and himself on a dapple grey, they took the road; but he soon became aware that Lord Douglas and his sons were following on their track, and likely to overtake them.

"Light down, light down, Lady Margaret," he
         said,
    "And hold my steed in your hand,
Until that against your seven brethren bauld,
    And your father, I mak a stand."

She held his steed in her milk-white hand,
    And never shed one tear,
Until that she saw her seven brethren fa',
    And her father hard fighting, who loved her
         so dear.

"O hauld your hand, Lord William!" she said,
    "For your strokes they are wondrous sair
True lovers I can get monie a ane,
    But a father I can never get mair."

It seemed as if the lady had begun to wish she had never left home. Devoted though she was to Lord William, the question pressed itself on her mind at this awful moment, " Would I not be a monster of cruelty to leave my father weltering in his blood, perhaps to die in agony and alone ? "   She must have been conscious that the service due to her aged sire could not be paid without increasing her lover's danger ; but, with true filial piety, she risked the perils of delay by lighting down and with her handkerchief

> . . . " dichting her father's bloody wounds,
> That were redder than the wine."

Thereat her lover waxed wroth, jealous too, because she seemed less heedful about his safety than her father's well-being.   With an unusual bitterness in his tone—

" O chuse, O chuse, Lady Margaret," he said,
 " O whether will ye gang or bide ? "

Dire necessity rather than the dictates of her heart shaped her choice when this painful alternative was placed before her :

> " I 'll gang, I 'll gang, Lord William," she said,
>   said,
> " For ye have left me nae other guide."

If at this terrible crisis the noble Lord seems unsympathetic and selfish, his conduct is soon made to appear in a less unfavourable light, and he becomes an object of tearful pity. His own strength was ebbing rapidly away; the minutes of his life were numbered; he felt that to-morrow's sun he would never see; and that a desolate future lay before the daughter of the house of Douglas, whose fate for evil, and nothing but evil, had been inextricably mixed up with his own. Never a word did he say about his deadly wounds. Had she not present misery enough without telling her of the fresh full cup that seemed to be in store for her, in lieu of the draughts of nuptial felicity of which they had that morning fondly dreamed? The fatal secret soon betrayed itself. Slowly they rode away from the spot where her seven brothers fell, and near which are still to be seen a group of large stones raised, tradition tells us, to commemorate their doom. Coming to the Douglas Burn, the lovers halted on its banks just before that stream joins the Yarrow. No more pathetic scenes are associated with doleful Yarrow's braes and river than those which ensued after they had taken temporary rest, and at the final close of their journey. They are described by the ballad minstrel with graphic force and appropriate feeling.

They lighted doun to tak a drink
  Of the spring that ran sae clear ;
And doun the stream ran his gude heart's
    blude,
  And sair she began to fear.

" Hold up, hold up, Lord William," she says,
  " For I fear that you are slain ! "

" Be not alarmed," he faintly replied—

" 'Tis naething but the shadow of my scarlet
    cloak,
  That shines in the water sae plain."

O they rade on, and on they rade,
  And a' by the licht o' the moon,
Until they cam to his mother's ha' door,
  And there they lichted doun.

" Get up, get up, lady mother," he says,
  " Get up, and let me in !—
Get up, get up, lady mother," he says,
  " For this nicht my fair lady I 've win."

From the pinnacle of exultation to the dust of
despair there was but a step :

" O mak my bed, lady mother," he says,
  " O mak it braid and deep !
And lay Lady Margaret close at my back,
  And the sounder I will sleep."

For a brief space the picture of her cheerless
loneliness after he was gone gave additional
gloom to the shadows that gathered around
his couch, and he could not but feel relieved
by knowing, before he breathed his last, that,
united to each other by love's sacred bonds, in
death they would not be long divided.

> Lord William was dead lang ere midnicht,
>   Lady Margaret lang ere day.

In contemplating their woful fate the feeling-
hearted minstrel ejaculates—

> And all true lovers that go thegither,
>   May they hae mair luck than they !

> Lord William was buried in St. Mary's Kirk,
>   Lady Margaret in Mary's quire ;
> Out o' the lady's grave grew a bonnie red
>   rose,
> And out o' the knight's a brier.

> And they twa met, and they twa plat,
>   And fain they wad be near ;
> And a' the warld micht ken richt weel,
>   They war twa lovers dear.

But the uncle, or other near relative of the
deceased lady, showed an animus against her

lover by maltreating the "bonnie brier bush" that grew above his dust:

> But bye and rade the Black Douglas,
>   And wow but he was rough!
> For he pull'd up the bonnie brier,
>   And flang 't in St. Mary's Loch.

ANNAN WATER.

A storm-tossed river, rolling broad and deep; a lady fair residing somewhere on its southern bank; her devoted lover, bent on seeing her that day, reaching the other side after "riding over field and fell, through muir and moss, and monie a mire." Such is the situation that is disclosed at the opening of our next ballad.

> " O, Annan water's wide and deep,
>   An' my love Annie 's wondrous bonnie;
> Shall I be laith to wat my feet
>   For her whom I love best of ony?

The question admitted of only one answer. But his grey mare, before " he wan the Gate-hope-slack," was so exhausted by its protracted journey as to be totally unfit to face the furious tide.

She was a meare, a richt gude meare ;
  But when she wan to Annan water,
She couldna hae ridden a furlong mair
  Had a thoosand merks been wadded at her.

The ferryman, however, is at hand :

  "O boatman, haste, put off your boat !
    Put off your boat for gowden monie !
  I cross the drumly stream this nicht,
    Or never mair I meet my honey."

Unlike the Highland boatman of Loch Foyle, his brother of the Border stream gives a negative response, not, it would seem, on account of the perilous flood, but because hostile influences had been brought to bear upon him by the lady's relatives or some jealous rival.

  " O ! I was sworn late, late yestreen,
    An' not by ae oath, but by many,
  For a' the gowd in braid Scotland
    I mauna tak ye through to Annie."

To the hoarse roar of the river itself, bidding the unfortunate knight beware, was added the warning of its guardian spirit :

  The side was steep, the bottom deep.
    Frae bank to brae the water pouring ;
  And the bonnie gray did shake for fear—
    She heard the water-kelpie roaring.

There must have been more than ordinary reasons why fair Annie's lover still persevered in his resolve to tempt the perils of the flood; though usually in such cases the interference of the kelpie came too late to save, its wail being the dirge of those whose doom had been sealed beyond remeid. Perhaps the ill-starred knight knew that Annie was about to be offered up at the matrimonial altar as the victim of a forced marriage, and believed that unless he—like young Lord Lochinvar under similar circumstances—interposed in the nick of time the sacrifice would be completed, and she would be lost to him for ever.

> O! he's put aff his dapper coat,
>   Wi' silver buttons glancin' bonnie;
> The waistcoat burstit aff his breast,
>   His heart leapt sae wi' melancholy.

> He's ta'en the ford at the stream tail;
>   I wat he swam baith stout and steady;
> The stream was broad, his strength did
>   fail—
>   He never saw his bonnie lady.

It seemed, as in the case of Edgar Ravenswood, that everything was against him. "The strong swimmer" had got within touch of the southern side, and might still have escaped as if by miracle, had not the bushes on the bank.

at which he convulsively snatched " in his
agony" given way. Yet whatever else proved
false, bonnie Annie remained true to him, and
deeply mourned his untimely fate.

" O wae betide the frush saugh wand,
    An' wae betide the brush o' brier,
They brak into my true love's hand,
    When strength did fail and limbs did tire.

" And wae betide thee, Annan stream,
    Thou art a deep and deadly river ;
But over thee I 'll build a bridge,
    That ye nae mair true love may sever."

YOUNG JOHNSTONE.

" Oh, thou invisible spirit of wine, if thou
hast no name to be known by, let us call thee
Devil !" So ejaculated Cassio, because, under
the maddening influence of strong drink, he
had played the part of a swaggering midnight
bravo, and thus forfeited the favour of his
commander, Othello. Some of the sufferers,
if not the actors, in the Border tragedy I am
about to notice might have indulged in a
similar soliloquy. Two youthful squires, just
returned from the hunting-field, are disclosed
drinking at the wine ; one of them, Johnstone.

is a cadet of the house of Annandale; the other,
probably a relative, is styled "The Young
Col'nel." But this seems to be an error due
to some reciter or copyist of comparatively
modern times, ignorant of the fact that there
was no rank in the army so designated at the
date of the tale. Professor Aytoun objects that
"the military title of Colonel is comparatively
recent, and does not assort with 'the belted
knights' and 'broad arrows' also specified in
the ballad;" he does not, however, suggest
any other reading, but I humbly propose Cow-
hill as a substitute for Col'nel. That is the
name of a Dumfriesshire estate, long possessed
by members of the Johnstone clan; and it
will be recollected that the hero of Allan
Cunningham's exquisite ballad, "The Mermaid
of Galloway," is termed "The Young Cowhill."

So loving do the young men seem, and so
confiding is one of them, Young Johnstone,
that he says to the other—

> " O gin ye wad marry my sister,
>   It 's I wad marry thine."

What but the malignant spirit of the wine-
cup could have inspired the insolent retort ?

> " I wadna marry your sister
>   For a' your houses and land ;
> But I 'll keep her for my leman
>   When I come oure the strand.

> ' I wadna marry your sister
> For a' your gowd and fee ;
> But I 'll keep her for my leman
> When I come oure the sea."

The blood of the Johnstone race was proverbially hot enough to resent an insult—"ready, aye ready," according to their motto. In this instance, apart from any artificial stimulus, it was sufficient to prompt the blow by which the perpetrator of the insult was made to expiate it with his life. "Ritted through" by the sword of Johnstone, the unfortunate Cowhill "word spak never mair." Off hurried the conscience-stricken homicide, but, I fancy, not caring to go to his own house, afraid, it may be, of being sought for there by the dead man's friends. Shelter of some kind he must needs obtain, as the gloom of midnight was settling down around him. The cruel irony of circumstance led him to his sister's bower; and, with the blood of her slaughtered lover on his hands, "he 's tirled at the pin." To the question—

> " Whare hae ye been, my dear brither,
> Sae late in coming in ?"

the guilty youth, afraid to answer truthfully, replied—

> " I hae been at the schule, sister,
> Learning young clerks to sing."

Half suspecting that something wrong had
occurred—

> " I 've dreamed a dream this nicht," she said,
>   " I wish it may be for gude !
> They were seeking you wi' hawks and hounds,
>   And the Young Cowhill was dead."

Thus indirectly arraigned, Johnstone acknow-
ledged his guilt—a confession of regret, if not
of penitence, trembling on his lips—

> " It 's seeking me wi' hawks and hounds,
>   I trow that weel may be,
> For I hae killed the Young Cowhill,
>   Though thy ain true love was he."

All the lady's sisterly affection then gave way
to a thirst for vengeance on the criminal, no
longer a brother to her, by whom her lover
had been foully done to death. With her
imprecations ringing in his ears, he hastened
away to seek refuge elsewhere. His victim
was the brother of his own true love. Would
she, if he appealed to her, not also say with
his own sister—

> " O dule and woe is me,
> I wish ye may be hanged on a hie gallows,
>   And hae nae power to flee."

His heart answered in the negative, and,

with more of hope than fear, he hastened to
her abode and asked for admission. With
true human instinct and genuine artistic skill
the author of the ballad proceeds to illustrate
the superiority of sexual love to sisterly affec-
tion. Parrying a question as to the cause of
her lover's late arrival, he at length reveals the
whole horrible truth, the lady having prompted
his confession by relating to him a dream she
had had parallel to that of the night-vision
seen by his sister: "Wae is me," because "ye
hae killed my ae brither;" but, "if thy ain
body be free, I care the less."

> " Come in, come in, my dear Johnstone,
>   Come in, and tak a sleep,
> And I will go to my casement,
>   And carefully will thee keep.
>
> " She hadna weel gane up the stair,
>   And entered in the tower,
> Till four-and-twenty belted knights
>   Cam riding to the door."

They were, as she understood at once, in quest
of Johnstone.

> " O, did you see a bloody squire,
>   A bloody squire was he?
> O, did you see a bloody squire
>   Come riding oure the lea?"

> " What colour were his hawks," she says,
>   " What colour were his hounds?
> What colour was the gallant steed
>   That bore him frae the bounds?"

Down till this stage there is no mention whatever of the fugitive having been accompanied by either dogs or falcons, and I suspect their introduction must be looked upon as a poetical flourish on the part of the story-teller; and certainly the verses relating to them are highly effective.

> " Bloody were his hawks and hounds,
>   And milk-white was his horse,"

said the leader of the troop.

> " Yes, bloody, bloody were his hawks,
>   And bloody were his hounds,
> And milk-white was the gallant steed
>   That bore him frae the bounds."

" That being so," replied the lady, with the view of putting them on a false scent, " you need not prosecute your journey further,

> " But light ye doun now, gentlemen,
>   And take some bread and wine;
> An the steed be swift that he rides on,
>   He 's past the brig o' Tyne."

" No, we must not tarry," said the chief, re-
solved to carry on the chase.

" We thank you for your bread, lady,
    We thank you for your wine ;
But I wad gie three thousand pounds
    That bloody squire were ta'en."

To account for what follows we must assume
that " the bloody squire " partly overheard and
misinterpreted this colloquy. The invitation of
the damsel, " Light ye doun now, gentlemen,"
followed by their mention of " three thousand
pounds " as the price they were ready to pay
for his capture, suggested to his mind the
horrible idea that the lady who was acting as
his guardian angel had, for sordid lucre's sake,
betrayed him into the hands of his enemies.
But the thought and the deed of blood which
it prompted must have been, I think, the work
of the wine-devil by which his brain had been
set on fire. Had he been in his sober senses
that dismal day and night, the tragedies which
render him the unhappy hero of this deeply
pathetic ballad could scarcely have occurred.
Perceiving him to be restless and anxious-look-
ing, the lady addressed him in soothing terms :

" Lie still, lie still, my dear Johnstone,
    Lie still and tak a sleep,
For they that sought for thee are gane,
    And carefully I'll thee keep."

He refused to be soothed or reassured, and
in the next verse he appears as the maddened
assassin of the lady to whom he owed his
heart's best love and a hiding-place from the
men who sought his life.

> But Johnstone had a little wee sword,
>   Hung low doun by his gair,
> And he's ritted it through his dear lady,
>   And wounded her sae sair.

" What aileth thee now?" murmured the
dying lady upbraidingly—

> " What aileth thee now, dear Johnstone,
>   What aileth thee at me?
> When I have watched to save thy life,
>   Deserved I this from thee?"

Was ever poor wretch in plight more pitiable
than young Johnstone when the awful reality
of the situation burst upon his mind? " Fool,
fool, fool!" the self-accused Othello exclaimed
under somewhat similar conditions. " Alack!
alack!" shrieked the Scottish gentleman,

> " I thought it was my deadly foe
>   Ye had trysted unto me,"

when you were acting as my truest friend.

> " O live, O live, my dear lady,
>   The space o' ae half hour,
> There's no a leech in a' Scotland
>   But shall be in thy bower."

She was beyond the reach of the best human skill. She felt that her case was hopeless, yet she would fain have lived for him; the love she bore her bosom's lord never having been stronger or brighter than now when dying by his hand :

" How can I live, my dear Johnstone,
  How can I live for thee?
O do ye na see my red heart's blude
  Run trickling doun my knee?

" But go thy way, my dear Johnstone,
  O go thy way and flee,
For never shall the word be said
  Ye cam to harm for me."

Even yet he was not "a-weary of the sun," and under the instinct of self-preservation he tore away from the side of his murdered sweetheart as she was breathing her latest sigh. But the Cowhill men were at hand to play the part of Nemesis.

He hadna weel been oot o' stable,
  And on his saddle sat,
Till four-and-twenty broad arrows
  Were thrilling in his heart.

THE MOTHER'S MALISON.

With his mother's curse on his head, Sweet Willie hies away after nightfall to May Margaret's bower, while a terrible storm raves over shore and river. Obviously the doure old dame did not relish the idea of acquiring that young damsel for a daughter-in-law; and Willie was desperately disobedient and rash when he rode off in defiance of his mother's warning.

> " O, gin ye gang to May Margaret
>   Without the leave o' me,
> Clyde's water 's wide and deep eneugh;
>   My malison droon thee."

> As he rade oure yon high, high hill,
>   And doun yon dowie glen,
> There was a roar in Clyde's water
>   Wad frichtened a hundred men.

Dashing into the flood, he crossed to the opposite bank in safety. Dearer to him than haven to the storm-tossed mariner was his sweetheart's bower as it dimly hove in sight. Shelter from the pitiless elements in love's fond embrace would soon, he thought, be his rapturous experience as, with trembling hand, he "tirled at the pin." No response, however, was made to his summons, and he could not force admission, as "doors were steekit and windows barred." When, shivering in the cold, he raised his voice and entreated her to give him access, he was greeted with a cruel repulse:

" I darena open the door to you,
　　Nor darena let you in,
For my mither she is fast asleep,
　　And I darena mak nae din."

" At least some pity on me shaw, if love it mayna be," prayed Lord Gregory's victim in Burns's pathetic lyric. So Sweet Willie appealed to the compassion of his lady fair, as his boots, " full o' Clyde's water, were frozen to the brim," and the midnight air was piercing him to the bones. " Tell me, tell me," he entreated, " o' some oot chamber where I this nicht may be."

" Ye canna win in this nicht, Willie,
　　Nor here ye canna be,
For I 've chambers oot nor in,
　　No ane, but barely three ;

" The tane o' them is fu' o' corn,
　　The tither is fu' o' hay,
The third is fu' o' merry young men—
　　They winna move off till day."

What a faithless and remorseless maiden this must be, all unworthy of Willie's devotedness ! If the reader should indulge in a reflection of this kind, it would be only natural. At a later stage, however, the balladist lets us know, indirectly, that the language just quoted came from Margaret's mother, who had imitated her daughter's voice, just as Lord Gregory's mother personated him when dismissing Annie o' Lochryan from his gates.

> " O, fare ye weel, May Margaret,
>   Sin' better maunna be ;
> I 've won my mother's malison
>   Coming this nicht to thee."

When attempting to recross the Clyde, " the rushing water took Willie frae his horse." Just at this agonising juncture, "up it waukened poor May Margaret oot o' her drowsy sleep," who said,

> " Come here, come here, my mother dear,
>   And read this dreary dream ;
> I dreamed my love was at our yetts,
>   But nane wad in let him."

Troth was he, replied the treacherous virago in effect, but lie still, and never fash your thumb ; it's " but twa quarters past " since he was here disturbing the house by his tirling at the pin. Lie still ! Impossible ! In a trice the young lady was striving with the torrent that was overbearing her true love. The first step took her up to the ankle :

> The neister step that she wade in
>   She waded to the knee ;
> Says she, " I wad wade farther in,
>   Gin I my love could see."

The neister step that she wade in
  She waded to the chin ;
The deepest pot in Clyde's water
  She got Sweet Willie in.

" You 've had a cruel mother, Willie,
  And I have had anither ;
But we shall sleep in Clyde's water,
  Like sister and like brither."

ERLINTON.

A bigly tower built to serve the purpose
of a jail; a beautiful young lady shut up
within it by her father, old Erlinton, and
watched by sisters six and brethren seven !
Yet the damsel thus treated does not appear
to have been unable to take care of herself,
and no particular crime was attributed to her
for which she deserved to dree such penance.
The balladist, in bringing the case of the fair
prisoner before us, blames her sire very
much : " I wat," he said, " he weird her in
a great sin," thus to make a celibate of one
whom neither nature nor grace ever intended
to be a nun. But her jailors " did their
spiriting gently." After a brief captivity she
managed to " break ward," and throw herself
into the arms of Willie—the man of all men
whose courtship of her was most repugnant

to her father. One night late, Willie knocked at the daughter's door and prayed for admission. There were obstacles in the way, she said : "In my bower there is a wake, and at the wake there is a wane," which she would elude in the morning early, and meet him at cock-crow in the bonnie green wood "whar blooms the brier." A bold, resolute, and self-reliant lady she must have been, presenting quite a contrast to her guardian sisters—a weak lot—whom she easily made submissive to her will.

She put on her back a silken gown,
  And on her breast a siller pin,
And she's ta'en a sister in ilka hand,
  And to the green wood she has gaen.

When they had walked in the forest "a mile, but barely ane," Willie met them, embraced his sweetheart fondly, and when her sisters frowned upon him for the freedom he took, he gently withdrew her from their company, kissed them courteously in turn, "and sent them hame !" Mounted on his horse, with the maiden behind him, they rode through the greenwood, she delighted with her escape and deliverer, he proud of his prize. If the curtain had fallen upon the youthful pair at this period, a prim-rose-path would have been theirs ; but he was destined to pass through streams of blood

before he could claim the fair damsel for his
bride.

They hadna ridden in the bonnie greenwood,
  Na not a mile, but barely ane,
When there cam fifteen o' the boldest knights
  That ever bare flesh, blude, or bane.

The foremost was an aged knight,
  He wore the grey hair on his chin,
Says, " Yield to me thy lady bright,
  An' thou shalt walk the woods within."

The speaker was none other than Erlinton ;
but Willie appears not to have known his
identity till the encounter which followed
was drawing near a close. Willie scorned to
surrender.

    " For me to yield my lady bright
      To such an aged knight as thee,
    People wad think I was gane mad,
      Or a' the courage flown frae me."

Challenged in a more boastful style by a
younger knight, Willie put the entire troop
at defiance, and, appealing to their sense of
manhood, tried to stipulate, without effect,
that they would " only fight him ane by ane."

    He lighted aff his milk-white steed,
      An' gaed his lady him by the head,
    Saying, " See ye dinna change your cheer
      Until you see my body bleed."

He set his back unto an aik,
  He set his feet against a stane,
An' he has fought these fifteen men,
  An' killed them a' but barely ane.

Need it be said that the one exception was Erlinton—the doure, foolish old knight, whose bigly-bower and nunnery-tower device led up to all this horrible carnage. The young warrior had pity on his grey hairs, and would rather have yielded up his own life than have done harm to his sweetheart's father. As for her "brethren seven," it may be safely inferred that they had kept out of danger, since they are not mentioned among the victims; if they had been numbered among the slain, such a pathetic culmination of the tragedy would not have been overlooked by its laureate. Willie left the aged knight "to carry the tidings hame," and, turning from a scene of bloody strife to one of gentle courtship.

He gaed to his lady fair,
  I wat he kissed her tenderlie ;
" Thou art mine ain love, I have thee bought,
  Now we shall walk the greenwood free."

JELLON GRÆME.

There are few ballads in the entire range of our Scottish minstrelsy that, for beauty of composition, exceed Jellon Græme; yet it is comparatively little known, and the unrelieved horror which pervades it, warp and woof, will keep it from ever becoming a general favourite. An unmitigated ruffian is the hero of the piece. After dishonouring the lady, Lillie Flower, he sends for the unfortunate victim of his sensual appetite, telling the messenger, as he sharpens his sword significantly, to bring her into his presence with all convenient speed.

> The boy he buckled his belt about,
>   And through the greenwood ran ;
> And he came to the lady's bower
>   Before the day did dawn.
>
> " O sleep ye, wake ye, Lillie Flower,
>   The red sun's on the rain."

Thus the page begins his address to the lady with a poetic gracefulness worthy of John Keats. He ends it with words of evil omen, that were fitted to overwhelm her in despair—

> " Ye 're bidden come to Silverwood,
>   But I doubt ye 'll never win hame."

When thus warned, why did she leave the shelter of her own domestic bowers ? Doubtless because Jellon Græme still exercised a

fascination over her, and she was still disposed
to put trust in the father of her unborn child.

> She hadna ridden a mile, a mile,
>   A mile but barely three,
> Ere she came to a new-made grave
>   Beneath a green aik tree.

> O, then up started Jellon Græme,
>   Out of a bush thereby,
> " Light down, light down now, Lillie Flower,
>   For it 's here that ye maun lie."

> She lighted aff her milk-white steed,
>   And kneeled upon her knee,
> " O mercy, mercy, Jellon Græme,
>   For I 'm no prepared to dee."

She entreated him by the pains of maternity
she was suffering, for the sake of the innocent
babe that was stirring in her womb, to look
upon her with pity.

> " O, should I spare your life," he says,
>   " Until that bairn were born,
> Full weel I ken your auld faither
>   Would hang me on the morn."

> " O, spare my life noo, Jellon Græme,
>   My faither ye needna dread ;
> I 'll keep my babe in gude greenwood,
>   Or in it I 'll beg my bread."

The monster lent a deaf ear to her cry, one fell sweep of the blade that he had whetted laid her lifeless on the sward—the Lillie Flower now "the flower of love lies bleeding" —blood-red all over, like a damask rose. But for the "bonnie lad bairn," ushered into the world by an accidental Caesarean operation, he felt compassion. Carrying the child home to Silverwood, he provided for him "nurses nine, three to sleep and three to wake and three to go between."

> And he bred up that bonnie boy,
>   Called him his sister's son ;
> And he thought no eye could ever see
>   The deed that he had done.

But the Providence that had witnessed the murder had an agent at hand who had been born to avenge it.

"So it fell upon a day" that father and son, when wearied with hunting, rested them in Silverwood, "beneath that green aik tree."

> And many were the green-wood flowers
>   Upon the grave that grew,
> And marvelled much that bonnie boy
>   To see their lovely hue.

Then the minstrel tells us that the curious

youth, as the fashion then went, gave his companion a series of riddles to solve—

> What 's paler than the primrose wan ?
>   What 's redder than the rose ?
> What 's fairer than the lily flower
>   On this wee knowe that grows ?

Taken thoroughly aback by this undesigned appeal to his conscience, the guilty man out "spak hastilie"—

> " Your mother was a fairer flower,
>   And lies beneath this tree.

> " Mair pale she was, when she socht my
>   grace,
>   Than primrose pale and wan ;
> And redder than rose her ruddy heart's
>   blude,
>   That down my braid sword ran."

> Wi' that the boy has bent his bow,
>   It was baith stout and lang,
> And through and through him, Jellon Græme,
>   He garred an arrow gang.

> Says, " Lie ye there now, Jellon Græme,
>   My malison gang you wi' !
> The place that my mother lies buried in
>   Is far too good for thee."

PART FIFTH.

MELO-DRAMATIC.

THE GAY GOSS-HAWK.

THE unnamed heroine of our next tale dwelt on the south side of the Border. She was the fairest flower in merry England; at all events so thought her Scottish lover, Lord William. When they flourished there was no postal service, and it was often a matter of both difficulty and danger for people living on opposite sides of the Tweed to hold communication with each other. Fortunately Lord William possessed a gay goss-hawk capable of rendering much greater service than any carrier pigeon of modern days; for this particular falcon had the gift of speech, and could therefore not only convey a written epistle under his wing, but also a message by word of mouth. Thus doubly equipped, and thoroughly well posted up by his master, the little feathered go-between flew off to his destination, and on reaching it had no difficulty in identifying a charming young lady, whom he saw going home from church, as Lord William's sweetheart.

> And when he flew to her castle,
>   He lighted on the ash ;
> And there he sat and there he sang
>   As she cam frae the mass.
>
> And when she went into the house,
>   He flew into the whin ;
> And there he sat and there he sang
>   As she gaed out and in.

Thus serenaded, the lady bade her bower women "pree the wine" by way of entertaining themselves, as she was going to "the west window to hear the birdie's sang." She opened the casement invitingly ; in fluttered the wonderful hawkie, and, shaking his wings, down fell a letter into her "white silk lap ;" while in language plainer than was ever spoken by the most eloquent of parrots he emphasised the contents of the missive by exhorting her to send a return message arranging for an interview with Lord William, failing which, the love-sick swain would "lay him doon and dee."

Quite unlike the Proud Margaret of another ballad, the damsel thus addressed sent back the bird with a fond, favourable reply, and bearing with him a wealth of love-tokens hid away under his plumage.

> " I send the rings from my white fingers,
>   The garlands off my hair ;
> I send him the heart that 's in my breast,
>   What wad my love hae mair ?
> And at the fourth kirk in fair Scotland,
>   You 'll bid him meet me there."

It is only from the strange arrangements she made to secure the appointed assignation that we become aware that her parents and brothers disapprove of Lord William's suit, that he durst not come to her openly, and that it was impossible for her to visit him in his own land. Placed in this dilemma, she resorts to a singular stratagem ; and as its nature is revealed, the memory recurs to the ill-starred daughter of the Capulets, and the potion which she took in order to simulate death.

> She 's gaen until her father dear,
>   As fast as she could hie.

> " An asking, an asking, my father dear,
>   An asking grant ye me,
> That if I die in merry England,
>   In Scotland you 'll bury me.

> " At the first kirk o' fair Scotland
>   Ye 'll cause the bells be rung,
> At the neist kirk o' fair Scotland
>   Ye 'll cause the mass be sung.
>
> " At the third kirk o' fair Scotland
>   Ye 'll deal the gowd for me,
> At the fourth kirk o' fair Scotland
>   It 's there ye 'll bury me."

Having obtained her father's consent to her
strange request, which he would probably look
upon as nothing worse than a whim, she
hurried on the plot to a further stage by pro-
ceeding to her bigly bower, swallowing the
potion which some village apothecary had
prepared for her, and then falling down seem-
ingly lifeless " beside her mother's knee."

> Then oot an' spak an auld witch-wife,
>   By the fire-side sat she,
>
> Says, " Drap the het lead on her cheek,
>   And drap it on her chin,
> And drap it on her rose-red lips,
>   And she will speak again."

This cruel experiment was tried without avail.
To all appearance the lady was beyond the
reach of surgery, or sorcery, or human aid in
any form. Nothing remained to the afflicted
father save to show his love for the child he

had so suddenly lost by carrying out the
promise he had made to her. He accordingly
ordered that her body should be borne away
forthwith to Scotland for burial.

> Then up arose her seven brothers,
>   And made for her a bier ;
> The boards were o' the cedar wood,
>   The plates o' silver clear.
>
> And up arose her seven sisters,
>   And made for her a sark ;
> The claith o' it was satin fine,
>   The steeking silken wark.

Bells were rung when the first North Country
kirk was reached ; at the second, mass was
sung ; at the third, a money largess was dis-
tributed among the mourners and onlookers.
When the fourth little sanctuary was brought
within sight, Lord William startled all pre-
sent by appearing upon the scene, and in
words that no one sought to challenge, he
commanded the pall-bearers to set down their
burden.

> " Set doon, set doon the bier," he said,
>   " Till I look on the dead ;
> The last time that I saw her face,
>   Her cheeks were rosy red."

Thus, with the utmost simplicity of language,
the balladist produces a series of telling dra-

matic effects, these going on till the curtain falls. The bier having been laid down, Lord William, trembling with the anxiety of long suspense,

> Rent the sheet upon her face
> A little abune the chin.

Heavens! how his heart must have leapt when

> Fast he saw her colour come,
> And sweet she smiled on him;

and oh how readily would he respond to his darling's request when, in accents feeble, but musical as those of angels, she cried—

> "O give me a chive of your bread, my love,
> And ae drap o' your wine,
> For I hae fasted for your sake
> These weary lang days nine."

Strengthened by a refreshing draught, she, with words of exultation and disdain, dismissed the mourners, who, when at home, had stood between her and her true love:

> "Gae hame, gae hame, my seven brothers!
> Gae hame, and blaw your horn!
> I trow ye wad hae gien me the skaith,
> But I 've gien you the scorn.

" I cam not here, to fair Scotland,
  To lie amang the dead,
But I cam here, to fair Scotland,
  Wi' my true love to wed."

And so, more fortunate than the lovers whose fate forms the theme of one of Shakespeare's saddest dramas, the Scottish Romeo won the English Juliet for wife, despite the national or personal feud by which their families were divided.

EARL RICHARD'S WEDDING.

This ballad is remarkable for its exuberant humour, combined with romantic incident; and the frequent recurrence of a musical cadence that renders it more than usually melodious. Out on a hunting expedition, Earl Richard meets with higher game in the green forest than he had looked for. This is " a weel-faured May," who yields to his embrace. She asks for his name, and receives an equivocal reply. He then mounts his horse, bids the lady good-bye, and prepares to ride off, leaving her deserted and forlorn. But she was possessed of courage and pride not less than of physical beauty ; recently, a pure " flower of the forest," she would not allow herself to be treated as a noisome weed, and insisted upon following the unknown knight, for whom, during their brief courtship, she had contracted an affection that was curiously alloyed with a feeling of contempt, and seemed on the point, at one time, of being swallowed up by hatred.

> She has kilted her green claithing
> A little abune the knee;
> And aye he rode, and aye she ran,
> Till they cam to the water o' Dee.

Arrived at the side of the river, Earl Richard showed a trace of humanity, if not of love, by saying to his fair follower, "Lassie, will ye ride?" She resolved to receive no favour at his hands short of wedlock: hence the nature of her reply—

> "Ye needna stop for me," she says,
> "I've learned it for my weal,
> That when I come to a deep water,
> I can swim like onie eel.

> "I learned it in my mother's bower,
> It's few hae learned it better,
> For be the water ne'er so wan,
> I'll swim 't like onie otter."

The ungallant lord was at his wit's end. With exalted ideas about his own rank, he felt that his social position would be compromised were he to marry the woman he had betrayed; and yet to see her run the risk of perishing in the river on his account was not to be thought of. The only mode for him to escape from his dilemma was, he fancied, a backward course on her part. Counselling her accordingly, he cried—

" Turn back, turn back, ye weel-faured May,
  My heart will break in three."

" And sae did mine," retorted the lady, when you took mean advantage of my weakness—

    " Sae did mine, on yon bonnie hill-side,
      When ye wadna let me be."

To her the river Dee seemed the Rubicon of her fate; and as her swimming ability vindicated the boast she had made of it, she breasted the billows in safety.

    And or that he was half-way through,
      On the other side was she.

    And there she sat and preened hersel',
      Sitting upon a stone;
    And there she sat to rest hersel',
      And see how he'd come on.

    To the pathetic inquiry made by the damsel—

    " How monie miles hae ye to ride?
      How monie hae I to gang?"

the disheartening reply, "thirty miles," was returned by Earl Richard.

For her to walk such a distance, wearied as she was by her long previous travel, was impossible, so she allowed the churlish fellow to ride homeward alone. But he was greatly mistaken if he supposed that he was now fairly quit of his importunate lover. If the old proverb, "Faint heart never won fair lady," be true, it was equally true in this case that a brave woman's heart effected a conquest in the face of countless difficulties. Refusing to accept defeat, "the weel-faured May" resolved, if possible, to enlist the services of Majesty on her side. She had no friend at court to plead for her, as the Duke of Argyll did for Jeanie Deans, but access to the presence of the sovereign was more easily obtained three hundred years ago than in the reign of George II.

The heroine of our tale secured the privilege by means of a gift to the official who kept watch at the gates of the royal palace.

> She took a ring frae her finger,
>   And gied it for her fee ;
> Says, "Tak ye that, my good porter,
>   The Queen maun speak wi' me."
>
> Noo she's gane ben through ae lang room,
>   And she's gane ben through twa ;

And she's gane ben a lang, lang trance,
   'Till she cam to the ha'.

Lo, the Queen, passing from her private chamber to greet her unknown visitor! This she does very graciously, as the suppliant kneels before her, and then proceeds to present her appeal—

" My errand it 's to thee, O Queen,
   My errand it 's to thee ;
There is a knight into your Court
   This day has robbed me."

To the queries of the Queen, " Is it your purse or your fee," or "the flower of your bodie," that you have been deprived of? the damsel gives a truthful answer. Settling the case there and then, Her Majesty thus delivered judgment :—

" O gin he be a single man,
   It 's he shall marry thee ;
But gin he be a married man,
   High hangit shall he be.

" There 's no a knight in a' my Court
   That thus has robbed thee
But ye 'll hae the troth o' his richt hand,
   Or else for your sake he'll dee,

"Though it were Earl Richard, my ain
    brother—
   Forbid that it should be."

It would seem that from the first the damsel
more than suspected that her betrayer stood
in that close relationship to the Queen; and
now said " the bonnie lass," with a sigh,

> " I wot the same man is he."

But the royal lady, requiring evidence of the
fact—

> " Noo could you wale the knight," she says,
>   " Amang a hundred men ? "
> " That wad I," said the bonnie lass,
>   " If there were hundreds ten."

A rich scene ensues when " the merry men " of
the Court are made to pass through the hall ;
Dickie, who was usually fond of showing
himself first, lingering suspiciously behind, and
trying to cheat the keen eye of our heroine
" by hauping on ae foot, and winking wi' ae
ee."   Penetrating through the poor disguise,
" Thou art the man," she said in effect, point-
ing to the pretended cripple.

> " Aha !" cried the bonnie lass,
>   " That same young man are ye."

To buy the lady off was his next scheme :

> He 's ta'en oot a hundred pound,
>   And told it in his glove ;
> Says, " Tak ye that, my bonnie lass,
>   And seek anither love."

" O na ! O na !" the lassie cried,
  " That 's what shall never be ;
I'll hae the troth o' your richt hand,
  The Queen she gave it me."

Richard durst not disobey the Queen's command, though he murmured against it grievously—

" I wish I had drank o' the water, sister,
  When I did drink your wine ;
Noo I maun wed a carle's daughter,
  And dree this shame and pyne."

With customary spirit the lady rebuked him—

" Maybe I am a carle's daughter,
  And maybe I am nane ;
But when we met in the greenwood,
  Why let you me not alane ?"

Submitting with a bad grace to his fate, the bridegroom condescended to ask the bride what sort of garments she wished to wear at the approaching ceremony, and whether she would walk to church or ride. Her reply was that she preferred a long robe to a common " syde," or short one, and meant to sit beside him on the saddle, as one horse could easily carry them both. By the stylish dress her own feminine vanity would be gratified,

and his exorbitant pride would be humbled
by the meanness of the equipage.

> When he was set upon the horse,
>   The lassie him behin',
> It 's cauld and eerie were the words
>   They twa had them between.
>
> And he has gien to her the ring—
>   A waefu' man was he ;
> And he has mounted at the kirk door,
>   Rade aff wi' his ladie.

Truly a humiliating spectacle, relieved by
ludicrous ingredients. The great and mighty
Earl Richard, full brother to Scotland's Queen,
wedded under such mean conditions, and
beginning his marriage-jaunt with his newly-
made Countess in the plebeian one-horse style
of Darby and Joan. And the pair did catch
it, the bride coming in for her full share of
opprobrium.

> And there was never word but ane
>   In a' that companie ;
> " O ill it suits a beggar's brat
>   At a gude knight's back to be !"

In acting the part forced upon her by her
husband and his aristocratic friends, she
acquired further means for punishing him,
which she employed with savage glee.

> Then by there cam a beggar wife,
>   The lady flung her a croun ;
> " Tell a' your neibours, when ye gae hame,
>   Earl Richard 's your gudeson."

He prayed her, as formerly, to have pity upon him, only, however, to get the old reproachful answer—

> " O haud your tongue, ye beggar's brat,
>   My heart will break in three !"
> " And sae did mine, on yon bonnie hill-side,
>   When ye wadna let me be."

> " And when they cam to Marykirk,
>   The nettles grew on the dyke,
> " Gin my carline mither were here," she
>   says,
>   " Sae weel she wad you pyke !"

> " Sae weel she wad you pyke," she says,
>   " She wad you pyke and pu';
> She wad boil ye weel, and butter ye weel,
>   And sup till she were fu'."

The glimpses of mendicant life here revealed by the balladist, would, I fancy, be familiar to Burns, as some of them are reflected in his glorious cantata that tells how

Ae night, at e'en, a merry core
  O' randie, gangrel bodies,
In Poosie-Nansie's held the splore,
  To drink their orra duddies,

the half-fuddled fiddler singing to his doxy :

At kirns and weddings we 'se be there,
And oh ! sae nicely 's we will fare ;
We 'll bouse about, till Daddie Care
  Sings whistle oure the lave o't.

Sae merrily 's the banes we 'll pyke,
And sun oursel's about the dyke,
And at our leisure, when ye like,
  We 'll whistle oure the lave o't.

Still continuing their journey, our young
married folks come to the water of Tyne, on
the merry-going mills of which the mischievous
wife bestows a benison that is meant to tell,
malison-like, on the head of her husband—

" Weel may ye clap, weel may ye gang,
  And better be your luck,
For I wot my minnie ne'er gaed by you,
  But she has filled her pock."

He 's drawn his hat out owre his face,
  And meikle shame thought he ;
She 's drawn her cap out owre her locks,
  And a licht laugh gied she.

One might have supposed that when they
arrived at Earl Richard's mansion the mortify-
ing termagancy from which he had suffered
all that weary day would cease, self-exhausted.
Not so, however; it was displayed in the
dining-room, and became more rampant than
ever in the bridal chamber. On seeing the
festive board luxuriously furnished, "out
spak the bonnie bride, and she spak never
blate,"—

"Gae tak awa the china plates,
    Gae tak them far frae me,
And bring to me a wooden dish,
    It's that I'm best used wi'.

"And tak awa thae siller spunes—
    The like I ne'er did see;
And bring to me the horn cutties,
    They're gude eneugh for me."

When they were dined, and served well,
    And a' men bound to rest,
Earl Richard and his bonnie bride
    In ae chamber were placed.

"O haud awa the linen sheets,
    They are o' Hollands fine;
And bring to me the linsey clouts
    That lang I hae laid in."

> " O haud your tongue, you beggar's brat,
>   My heart will break in three ;"
> " And sae did mine, on yon bonnie hill-side,
>   When ye wadna let me be."

The climax of tormenting vulgarity was reached by the Countess when she called for two pokes of meal—one for her head, and the other for her feet—and told the Earl to reserve the Holland sheets for himself. His stock of endurance was now exhausted, and in a paroxysm of rage he exclaimed—

> " Haud far awa, ye carline's brat,
>   Haud far awa frae me ;
> It doesna suit a beggar's brat
>   My bed-fellow to be."

The lady replied by firing off one of her old retorts ; and just as the reader is beginning to fear that the laughter-provoking melo-drama is about to be rounded off by a doleful scene of blood and murder, a kind-hearted brownie, with whom we have met before, interposes to scold the quarrelsome couple, and to disclose a secret which operates like a charm on the rank-worshipping heart of the hero, and reconciles them to each other.

> It 's up then spak the Billy Blin
>   From the corner where he lay ;
> " What gars you twa keep havering on
>   Sae lang or it be day ?"

" Let a body rest," said the Billy Blin,
  " The ane may serve the ither,
The Earl o' Stockford's ae daughter,
  And the Queen o' Scotland's brither."

" O, fair fa' you, ye Billie Blin,
  And weel aye may ye be ;
For I 've socht her lang, and I hae her noo,
  And my ain dear wife is she."

How far the lady knew before this revelation
that she was of noble birth, the author of this
exquisite ballad does not say.

FAIR ANNIE.

" Learn to mak your bed, Annie,
  And learn to lie your lane ;
For I am going ayont the sea,
  A braw bride to bring hame.

" Wi' her I 'll get baith gowd and gear,
  Wi' thee I ne'er got nane ;
I got thee as a waif woman,
  I 'll leave thee as the same."

The speaker is Lord Thomas, the lady he
addresses Fair Annie, " by habit and repute "
his wife, who had borne to him seven sons ; but
as their marriage had not been sanctioned by
Holy Church, he resolves to desert her, and,

adding insult to injury, he asks her to make all due arrangements for welcoming his new " bright bride," when, a twelvemonth and a day hence, he brings her home. Annie, not less meek than beautiful, agrees to obey the mandate of her hard-hearted master. Accord-dingly, when the proper time arrived.

> She 's drest her sons i' the scarlet red,
>   Herself in the dainty green ;
> And though her cheek looked pale and wan,
>   She weel micht hae been a queen.

> She called upon her eldest son ;
>   " Look yonder what you see,
> For yonder comes your father dear,
>   Your stepmother him wi'."

Fair Annie manifested a humility and generosity that seem superhuman, when, addressing her false lord and her successful rival, she says—

> " You 're welcome hame, my ain gude lord,
>   To your halls but and your bowers ;
> You 're welcome hame, my ain gude lord,
>   To your castles and your towers ;
> Sae is the bricht bride you beside,
>   She 's fairer than the flowers."

Thanking the " fair maiden " who spoke so

courteously, the bride put a question to her husband that remained unanswered.

> " O what'n a maiden 's that," she says,
>   " That welcomes you and me ?
> She is sae like my sister Anne
>   Was stoun o' the bower frae me."

A touching picture of self-abnegation was presented when Annie maintained a semblance of gaiety, though her heart was like to break, as she waited like a menial upon the guests.

> O she has served the lang tables
>   Wi' the white bread and the wine ;
> But aye she drank the wan water,
>   To keep her colour fine.
>
> And as she gaed by the first table,
>   She leugh amang them a' ;
> But ere she reached the second table,
>   She loot the tears doon fa'.
>
> She 's taen a napkin, lang and white,
>   And hung it upon a pin,
> And it was a' for to dry her een,
>   As she gaed oot and in.

By-and-bye her native sweetness gives way under the tremendous strain to which it had been subjected. The meek matron of the day appears at nightfall, after the feast is over, as a mad fury bent on doing something desperate to the wedded pair, or to herself, or to her dishonoured progeny.

> When bells were rung, and mass was sung,
>   And a' men boun' to bed,
> The bride but and the bonnie bridegroom
>   In ae chamber were laid.

Will Annie, dagger in hand, steal into the bed-chamber on murderous errand bent—as some other ballad heroines had done under similar conditions—and then, after inflicting vengeance on its inmates, use the gory weapon against herself? To this tragical issue the crisis seemed tending, but a mediator was at hand. Quite opportunely "an aged man stood behind the door," to whom Annie told her sorrowful tale, and from whom she received counsel as to what she ought to do. As advised by the veteran sage,

> She's taen a harp into her hand,
>   Went to their chamber door ;
> And aye she harpit and aye she mourn't,
>   Wi' the saut tears falling o'er.

Then the fair minstrel gave vent to her agonising feelings by singing this terrible imprecation—

" O seven full fair sons hae I borne
  To the gude lord o' this place,
And O that they were seven young hares,
  And them to rin a race,
And I mysel' a gude grey-hound,
  And I wad gie them chase.

" O seven full fair sons hae I borne
  To the gude lord o' this ha',
And O that they were seven rattons,
  To rin frae wa' to wa',
And I mysel' a gude grey cat,
  And I wad worry them a'."

" My goun is on," said the new-come bride,
  " My shoon are on my feet,
And I will gae to Annie's chamber,
  And see what gars her greet."

During the midnight interview of these ladies
fair, the plot takes a turn that is not less sur-
prising than agreeable :

" O wha was't was your father, Annie,
  And wha was't was your mother ?
And had ye ony sister, Annie,
  Or had ye ony brother ? "

" The Earl o' Richmond was my father,
  His lady was my mother,
And a' the bairns, beside mysel',
  Was a sister and a brother."

" O, weel befa' your sang, Annie,
　　I wat ye hae sung in time ;
Gin the Earl o' Richmond was your father,
　　I wat sae was he mine."

" Come to your bed, my sister dear,
　　It ne'er was wranged for me,
I had but ae kiss o' his merry mou',
　　As we cam o'er the sea.

" There were five ships o' gude red gowd
　　Cam o'er the seas wi' me ;
It 's twa o' them will tak' me hame,
　　And three I 'll leave wi' thee.

" Three o' them I 'll leave wi' thee,
　　For tocher gat ye nane ;
But thanks to a' the Powers in Heaven,
　　That I gang maiden hame."

One scarcely knows which of the two sisters most to admire. Lord Thomas, who had gained the love of both, was worthy of neither. In the absence of any further information, we can only hope that he at length realised the value of fair Annie, apart from her new golden tocher, and that they afterwards lived happily together.

HYNDE ETIN.

Standing in her bower-door, Lady Margaret hears the sound of a hunting-horn floating from the direction of Elmond wood. Her destiny through all time is determined by that tuneful strain. Though late at e'en, she hied away to the gay green grove, as if drawn thither by an irresistible spell. Like the damsel who paid a lonesome visit to Carterhaugh on Hallowe'en, she began to pick blossoms from the tasselled shrubs that grew around. After being courteously challenged for using such freedom, not as in the case of Janet, by a fairy mannikin, but by a stalwart youth named Hynde Etin, her father's page, she yielded to his embraces, and for twelve long years afterwards they lived together, having for home the fairest bower that could be fashioned in the deepest recesses of the forest. They had six sons, the eldest of whom went out one day to hunt with his father.

When they were in the gay green wood,
   They heard the mavis sing;
When they were up aboon the brae,
   They heard the kirk bells ring.

The boy, having obtained leave to put a question to his father, says—

" My mother's cheeks are aft-times wat—
　　It 's seldom they are dry ;
What is 't that gars my mother greet,
　　And sab sae bitterlie ? "

" Nae wonder she should greet," answered
Hynde Etin, " nae wonder she should pine,"

" For it is twelve lang years and mair
　　She 's seen nor kith nor kin ;
And it is twelve lang years and mair
　　Since to the kirk she 's been.

" Your mother was an Earl's daughter,
　　And come of high degree ;
She micht hae wedded the first in the land,
　　Had she no been stown by me ;

" For I was but her father's page,
　　And served him on my knee,
And yet my love was great for her,
　　And sae was her's for me.

" But we 'll shoot the laverock in the lift,
　　The buntlin on the brae,
And ye 'll carry them hame to your mother,
　　See if she 'll merrier be."

But the lady's grief was too deep-seated to be
alleviated by presents of any kind, even
though given as tokens of unwavering truth
by the father of her children. " It fell upon

another day " that he again went a-hunting—
this time alone. Taking the opportunity of
Etin's absence, the eldest son repeated to his
mother the statement made to him by her
husband. She confirmed the tale, and it
fostered in her heart a consuming desire to
hear once more the music of the bells, and
make up her peace with the Church and with
the parents she had deserted. For the pur-
pose of bringing about these precious results,
Lady Margaret set out for her father's castle
"in the opening haugh," first sending her
eldest boy on before with three rings, and in-
structions how to use them.

> "The first ye 'll gie to the proud porter,
>   And he will let you in ;
> Ye 'll gie the next to the butler boy,
>   And he will show you ben ;
>
> " You 'll gie the third to the minstrel
>   That 's harping in the ha',
> And he 'll play good luck to the bonnie boy
>   That comes frae the greenwood shaw."

Young Etin, by acting as required, gained
ready access to the presence-chamber.

> And when he cam before the Earl,
>   He louted on his knee ;
> The Earl he turned him round about,
>   And the saut tear blint his e'e.

" Kneel no longer." said the old Lord.

> " Win up, win up, thou bonnie boy,
>   Gang frae my companie ;
> Ye look sae like my dear daughter,
>   My heart will burst in three."

"That this should be sae," exclaimed the youth,

> " A wonder it is nane
>   If I look like your dear daughter,
> For I am her eldest son."

" Where may my Margaret be ? " was the next query of the wondering and anxious Earl, his heart bounding with delight when he was told

> " She 's standing een noo before the yett,
>   And my five brothers her wi'."

Next minute Margaret was kneeling before her enraptured father. Raising her up, he declared that she would dine with him that joyful day. Margaret, while glad beyond measure to receive her father's forgiveness, could not feel at ease while her husband's fate still hung in the balance.

> " I may not eat o' the wheaten bread,
>   Nor yet drink o' the wine,
> Until I see my dear husband
>   That I hae left behin'."

A band of rangers bold, commissioned by their noble master, searched the forest through for Hynde Etin, with orders to bring him to the castle when discovered. They lighted upon him, all forlorn, pacing distractedly beside his now solitary bower. When he recognised the Earl's foresters he thought his doom was sealed, and, welcoming them as messengers of death, he said—

> " O let him tak frae me the head,
>   Or hang me on a tree ;
> For since I 've lost my ain true love,
>   My life 's nae worth to me."

Scarcely could he credit the testimony of his ears when told by the rangers that they would do him no harm, that his lady, pardoned by her father, was waiting impatiently for him with their sons at the castle, and that the Earl's forgiveness extended to him also. Hynde Etin was greeted courteously by the Earl, affectionately by Lady Margaret, while doubtless the rough, forest-bred boys would be filled with wonder as they realised, bit by bit, the nature of the new world that had burst so suddenly on their view. The long-delayed dinner was now partaken of, and a luxurious family feast it was, "the fatted calf," or a red deer equivalent of that proverbial dainty, together with wine of the best, enriching the social board. Yet something was needed to give contentment to the guests.

> As they were at the dinner set,
>   The young boy thus spak he :
> " I wish we were at haly kirk,
>   To get our christendie."

To the sanctuary they all went, the mother sinking down on the threshold for very shame.

> Then out and spak the parish priest,
>   And a sweet smile gied he :
> " Come ben, come ben, my lily flower,
>   And bring your babes to me ;"
> And he has taen and sained them a',
>   And gien them christendie.

What a rare specimen of chivalry and piety, of paternal love and Christian charity, is presented by this grand old Earl ! More worthy of the minstrel's praise is he than even the doughty knight who performs prodigies of valour, and carries with him trophies of victory from the tented field.

GEORDIE.

There was a battle in the North,
    It wasna' far frae Fordie ;
And they hae killed Sir Charles Hay,
    And they laid the wyte on Geordie.

In this way a spirited little ballad is begun, which strikingly illustrates the devotedness of wifely affection on the part of Geordie's spouse, her character and conduct presenting a pleasing contract to those of the Baroness of Brackley, as set forth in a preceding tale. It is supposed that the affray in which Sir Charles Hay lost his life took place during the reign of James V., and that the Geordie blamed for it was none other than George Gordon, Earl of Huntley ; but the events are not recorded in history. Consigned to prison, adjudged to death by the hands of the executioner, Geordie wrote a letter to his lady, praying her to intercede on his behalf. The news appalled her. Red and rosy was she on recognising her good lord's hand ; but "she hadna' read a word but twa" till her cheeks grew lily pale. Only for a minute or two, however, did she indulge in unavailing grief. Turned at once into a heroine by the terrific crisis she was called upon to face, she, checking her sobs, and brushing aside her tears, cried—

" Gae get to me my gude grey steed,
　My menzie a' gae wi' me,
For I shall neither eat nor drink
　Till E'nbrugh toun shall see me."

" Too late ! " a timid woman would have said, and given herself up to despair, for on the arrival of the Countess in the Scottish capital,

First appeared the fatal block,
　And syne the axe to heid him,
And Geordie comin' doun the stair,
　And bands o' airn upon him.

But though he was chained wi' fetters
　　strang,
　O' airn and steel sae heavy,
There wasna ane in a' the Court
　Sae braw a man as Geordie.

So long as there is life there is hope. "Come along, my gallant clansmen ; ' keep you ready,' in case of need, while I pray for mercy at the hands of our Sovereign Liege."

O she 's doun on her bended knee,
　I wat she 's pale and wearie :
" O pardon, pardon, noble King,
　And gie me back my dearie.

" I hae born seven sons to Geordie dear,
    The seventh ne'er saw his daiddie ;
O pardon, pardon, noble King,
    Pity a waefu' lady."

But James V. was in the same unrelenting
mood that made him proof to all Johnnie
Armstrong's petitions for mercy :

" Gae bid the heiding-man mak haste,"
    The King replied fu' lordly.

Then the fair suppliant, kneeling at his feet,
sought to move him by worldly considerations,
seemingly in vain :

" O noble King, tak' a' that 's mine,
    But gie me back my Geordie."

Since neither appeals to the King's clemency
nor to his love of wealth are of any avail, we
must see what effect the threat of force will
have upon him. So resolving, the noble lady
motioned to her menzie—the men-at-arms
who accompanied her from home :

The Gordons cam and the Gordons ran,
    And they were stark and steady ;
And aye the word amang them a'
    Was, " Gordons, keep you ready !"

At this juncture, when the royal forces round

the scaffold were menaced with a movement
for the rescue of the doomed Earl, good ad-
vice was received by the King from one of
his venerable nobles, which, fortunately, his
Majesty acted upon—

> "Gar her tell doun five thousand pounds,
>   And gie her back her dearie."

Five thousand pounds! Where was the money
to come from? The Countess could not, out
of her own resources, improvise anything like
such a sum ; but there were men of means
and liberality within hearing, who, out of ad-
miration for her bravery and magnanimity,
enabled her to make up the full amount.   It
does one's heart good to find the lady's nobility
of soul so generously recognised in this way,
and happy must have been the ministrel when
he could close his tale, that opened so dole-
fully, with the verses that follow—

> Some gae her merks, some gae her crouns,
>   Some gae her dollars many ;
> And she's tell'd doun five thousand pounds,
>   And she's gotten again her dearie.

> She blinkit blithe in her Geordie's face,
>   Says, "Dear hae I bought thee, Geordie ;
> But there sud hae been bluidy bouks on the
>   green,
>   Or I had tint my lordie ! "

> He claspit her by the middle sma',
>   And he kissed her lips sae rosy :
> " The fairest flower o' womankind
>   Is my sweet, bonnie lady."

CAPTAIN OGILVIE.

For the sake of variety I shall now bring under the reader's notice a group of ballads which, while still amatory and romantic, are more of a domestic nature than those previously dealt with in this section. The first relates to a runaway match (a favourite theme with the ancient rhymers), brought about by the circumstance of a patrician damsel, Lady Jean, daughter of the Duke of Gordon, having become so desperately enamoured of a poor military officer, Captain Ogilvie, that " awa wi' him she wad gae." The lady and her two sisters, Elizabeth and Margaret, feeling life in Castle Gordon to be rather monotonous, had passed a season in Aberdeen, where Jean made an acquaintance with Captain Ogilvie, which soon ripened into warm heart affection on both sides. The old Duke, hearing of the projected mesalliance, hurried down in great dismay towards the granite city, with the view, if possible of preventing it—

> They werena a mile frae Aberdeen,
>   A mile but only threen,
> Till he met wi' his twa daughters walking,
>   But awa was Lady Jean.

A question from him as to her whereabouts drew forth the reply—

> ' O pardon us, honoured father !
>   O pardon us," they did say,
> " Lady Jean is wi' Captain Ogilvie,
>   And awa wi' him she will gae."

At Aberdeen, whither the old nobleman went, he saw the young officer " training up his men," charged him with the abduction of Lady Jean, and declared he would make him swing for it on the gallows-tree. Accordingly the Duke laid his sore grievance before the King by letter, and craved sentence of death upon the culprit. But his Sovereign Highness, declining to abuse the Royal prerogative in such a merciless fashion, simply ordered Ogilvie to be reduced to the ranks, and that in itself was a cruel punishment.

> Word cam to Captain Ogilvie,
>   In the chamber where lay he,
> To cast off the gold lace and scarlet,
>   And put on the single livery.

The poor fellow submitted without a murmur,

though he must have felt sick at heart on his wife's account. Nursed in the lap of luxury, with royal blood in her veins, and a fitting match for the noblest and wealthiest in the realm, she was now brought face to face with poverty and toil. For himself, had he stood alone, he would have been content to suffer.

> " If this be for bonnie Jeanie Gordon,
>   This penance I 'll tak wi';
> If this be for bonnie Jeanie Gordon,
>   All this will I dree."

> Lady Jean had not been married
>   Not a year but three,
> Till she had a babe on every airm,
>   Anither on her knee.

All that long period she and her husband had been travelling about as vagrants. Is it wonderful that the patience of the lady gave way at last? When looking at her children, and thinking of their hardships, not less than her own, her thoughts turned homewards with a sigh, and the pathetic cry—

> " O but I 'm weary o' wandering !
>   O but my fortune is bad !
> It sets na the Duke o' Gordon's daughter
>   To follow a soldier lad."

When they cam to the Hieland hills,
    Cauld was the frost and snow;
Lady Jean's shoon they were a' torn,
    She could nae further go.

Again on the inclement air rose the sorrowful
wail of Lady Jean—

" O wae to the hills and the mountains !
    Wae to the wind and the rain !
My feet is sair wi' ganging barefit,
    Nae further am I able to gang.

" Wae to the hills and the mountains !
    Wae to the frost and the snow !
My feet is sair wi' ganging barefit,
    Nae further am I able for to go.

" O if I were at the glens o' Foudlen,
    Where hunting I hae been,
I could find the way to bonnie Castle Gordon,
    Without either stockings or sheen."

The scene now shifts to her father's castle ; at
its gates appear the ex-captain and his wife,
sorely travel-stained, and carrying their babies
three. The porter, recognising Lady Jean,
loudly announced her arrival. Thereupon
the Duke exclaimed—

" O you 're welcome, bonnie Jeanie Gordon,
   You are dear welcome to me,
You are welcome, dear Jeanie Gordon,
   But awa wi' your Captain Ogilvie !"

Thus rebuffed, the gallant soldier turned on his heel, and ere long broad seas were rolling between him and all that he cared about on earth. When his fortunes were at the lowest they rose in leaps and bounds. The totally unlooked-for message reached him " to come and heir his brother's land."

" Come home, you pretty Captain Ogilvie
   And heir your brother's land ;
Come home, you pretty Captain Ogilvie,
   Be Earl of Northumberland."

" O what does this mean ?" says the Captain ;
   Where 's my brother's children three ? "
" They are a' dead and buried,
   And the lands are ready for thee."

So then, after all, Jeanie has for husband a nobleman of well-nigh as good rank as her own sordid and haughty sire. Recrossing the rolling deep,

He soon cam to Castle Gordon,
   And doun on the green cam' he ;
The porter gave out with a loud shout,
   " Here comes Captain Ogilvie !"

Mark how, in greeting him, the ignoble Duke,
true to his character, changed his tune —

> "You 're welcome, pretty Captain Ogilvie ;
>   Your fortune 's advanced I hear,
> Nae stranger can come into my gates
>   That I do love sae dear."

With becoming dignity the young Earl replied—

> " Sir, the last time I was at your gates
>   You would not let me in ;
> I 'm come for my wife and children,
>   No friendship else I claim."

The sly old Duke persists, and holds out
tempting offers, which are scornfully refused
by his son-in-law, noble by nature, not less
than by rank—

> " Come in, pretty Captain Ogilvie,
>   And drink o' the beer and the wine,
> And thou shalt have gold and silver
>   To count till the clock strikes nine."

> " I 'll hae nane o' your gold and silver,
>   Nor nane o' your white monie,
> But I 'll hae bonnie Jeanie Gordon,
>   And she shall now go wi' me."

The ballad finishes gloriously—

Then she cam tripping doun the stair,
  With the tear into her e'e,
One babie was at her fit,
  Anither upon her knee.

" You 're welcome, bonnie Jeanie Gordon.
  Wi' my young familie,
Mount and go to Northumberland,
  There a Countess thou shalt be."

GLASGOW PEGGIE.

In the opinion of Patie, the hero of Allan Ramsay's famous pastoral, there was no maid living who could compare with Peggie, the beautiful shepherdess whose love he won at "the wauking o' the fauld." To another damsel of the same name we are introduced in a fine old ditty. She dwelt, not in rural Habbie's Howe, but in Glasgow, where she was "the toast of a' the town." She was perfection itself in the eyes of a handsome young mountaineer, who had resolved to carry her off from a host of Lowland swains, who, like himself, had been captivated by her charms. It has so happened, too, that their adventures form the theme of an excellent song by the author of "The Gentle Shepherd," the opening line of which he has borrowed from the lay of his fellow-minstrel—

The Lowland lads think they are fine,
   But the Hieland lads are brisk and gawsy.
And they hae come doon to Glasgow toun,
   To steal awa a bonnie lassie.

And the bold chief of the tartaned troop made no secret of his designs. He avowed them in the hearing of the parent pair, both of whom protested that they would not allow their dear bairn to cast in her lot with "a Hieland fellow." He says—

"O I wad gie my bonnie black horse,
   And sae wad I my gude grey naigie,
That I were a hundred miles in the North,
   And nane wi' me but my bonnie Peggie."

But up then spak the auld gudeman,
   And wow but he spak wondrous saucie :
" Ye may steal awa our cows and ewes,
   But ye shanna get our bonnie lassie."

Donald, knowing that the lassie herself was on his side, was no less obstinate—

" I hae got cows and ewes enow,
   I 've got gowd and gear already ;
Sae I dinna want your cows and ewes,
   But I will hae your bonnie Peggie."

Then " the auld gudewife, wondrous yellow" with rage, dared the damsel, " Now, since I 've

brocht ye up this length," to move a step.
But, like Bonnie Lizzie Bailie, Peggie had re-
solved to run off with her lover at all risks;
and so she, in spite of the maternal interdict,
announced her determination to follow her
Hieland laddie " through frost and sna',"
" owre moss and muir," and " mountains
many."

> He 's set her on his bonnie black horse,
>   Himsel' upon his gude grey naigie;
> And they hae ridden owre hills and dales,
>   And he 's awa' wi' his bonnie Peggie.

Quite a sensation was caused, not only in
urban circles, but over a wide outlying dis-
trict, by this daring abduction case and its
romantic development.

> As they rade out frae Glasgow toun,
>   And by the side o' Antermony,
> There they met the Earl o' Hume,
>   Wi' him his auld son riding bonnie.

The sight was a sad surprise to Lord Hume;
he could not but mourn that

> " The bonniest lass in a' Glasgow toun
>   Is aff this day with a Hieland laddie."

As the pair passed through " auld Drymen
toun," its rural nymphs, turning up their

noses, " leuch and lookit saucy," and agreed in thinking, with the noble Earl, that the surprising beauty of the lady (which, strange to say, they readily admitted) ought to have secured for her a much better husband than this adventurer from the North.

But Glasgow Peggie had made her choice, and had the best of reasons for being satisfied with it. Wedded after a very primitive fashion not yet obsolete, the lovers, on the approach of night, took needful rest.

> Gude green hay was Peggie's bed,
>   And brakens were her blankets bonnie,
> Wi' his tartan plaid beneath her head,
>   And she 's lain doun wi' the Hieland
>   laddie.

Not in any regretful mood, I fancy, but merely as a casual, natural reflection, the lady remarked next morning—

> "There 's mair than ae bed in my father's
>   house,
>   Sheets and blankets, and a' things ready;
> And wadna they be angry wi' me,
>   To see me lie sae wi' a Hieland laddie ? "

The reply of Donald reveals a well-kept secret, inasmuch as he makes known to his bride, for the first time, that, even from a worldly point of view, the old folks at home had no reason to be angry with her on his account. Doubtless the plenishing of her father's house was abundant and rich ; but

> " Dinna ye see yon nine score o' kye
>   Feeding on yon hill sae bonnie ?
> They 're a' mine, and they 'll sune be thine,
>   And what needs your mother be sorry,
>   Peggie ? "

> " See ye no a' yon castles and towers,
>   The sun shines on them a' so bonnie ;
> It 's I am Donald, the Lord of Skye—
>   I think I 'll mak ye as blithe as ony."

Summing up, the minstrel seems rather to depreciate unduly the antecedents of the lady when he says—

> A' that Peggie left behind
>   Was a cot-house and a wee kail-yardie,

though we must all concur with him when he adds—

> Noo, I think, she is better by far
>   Than though she had got a Lowland lairdie.

RICHIE STORIE.

In another ballad with a similar plot, probably written by the same author, we are told how the youngest daughter of the Earl of Wigton was courted by a man of professedly low degree, who, after their marriage, proved to be a wealthy cavalier. I quote the closing verses, which contain the pith of a very beautiful old ditty, and which is rendered all the more interesting from the circumstance that it forms the groundwork of the popular modern song, "Huntingtower."

O he 's gane on the braid, braid road,
    And she 's gane through the broom sae
        bonnie,
Her silken robes down to her heels,
    And she 's awa wi' Richie Storie.

This lady gaed up the Parliament stair,
    Wi' pendles in her ears sae bonnie ;
Mony a lord lifted his hat,
    But little did they ken she was Richie's
        lady.

Up then spak the Earl o' Hume's lady :
    " Wasna ye richt sorry, Annie,
'To leave the lands o' bonnie Cumbernauld,
    And follow Richie Storie, Annie ? "

"O what need I be sorry, madam?
  O what need I be sorry, madam?
For I 've got them that I like best,
  And were ordained for me, madam."

" Cumbernauld is mine, Annie,
  Cumbernauld is mine, Annie;
And a' that 's mine it shall be thine,
  As we sit at the wine, Annie."

THE DUKE OF ATHOL'S NURSE.

Just such a false nurse as figured in the
tragedy of " Lammikin" was the heroine of
this ballad. Sighing for " ae sight" of her
Johnnie, declaring that to obtain her desire
she would readily forfeit her half-year's fee,
who should start up before her but her dearly-
beloved swain?

" O here is your Johnnie just by your side,
  What hae ye got to say to your dearie?
O here is my hand, but anither has my
    heart,
  And I daurna mair come near ye."

The damsel, upbraiding Johnnie for his per-
fidious conduct, exacted a promise from him
to meet her once again before they parted

for ever. She fixed as the place of tryst a
little hostelry near by.

> " Yese do ye doon to yon change house,
>   And there bide till the dawing,
> And as sure as I aince had a love for you,
>   I'll come there and I'll clear your
>   lawing.

> " Ye'll spare not the wine, though it be
>   very fine,
>   And ye'll not leave it early ;
> But aye ye'll drink to the bonnie lassie's
>   health
>   That's to clear your lawing fairly."

Johnnie acted up to orders ; but though he
tippled away "till the sentinel cock an-
nounced the approach of day," he, contrary to
the expectation of the Duke's nurse, kept
himself comparatively sober. As the hour
fixed for their interview had arrived,

> He's gaen him to a little shot window,
>   To see if she were coming ;
> And there he spied twelve weil-airmed
>   men,
>   That owre the hill were running.

Poor Johnnie now realised the nature of the
plot that had been laid for him.

" Where shall I rin, or where shall I gang,
   Or where now shall I lay me ?
For she that was aince my ain true love
   Has sent her kin to slay me."

In his straits he appealed to the landlady, a
thrifty as well as kindly old dame, who had
risen early to bake bread for the family break-
fast.

" Now haud your tongue," said the wylie
      gudewife,
  " Your life sall no be taken ;
Gae put ye on my ain body claes,
   And set ye to the baking."

A device similar to one resorted to by Wallace
on a memorable occasion was thus suggested
and acted upon.   How it succeeded I shall
let the balladist tell in his own words :

Sae loudly as they rapped at the yett,
   Sae loudly they were ca'ing :
" O had ye a young man here yestreen ?
   We hae come to pay his lawing."

" There was a young man here yestreen,
   But he gaed ere the dawing ;
He had but ae pint, and he paid it or he
      went ;
   What hae you to do wi' the lawing ?"

" Show us the room the young man lay in,
    And maybe we 'll come near him."
They stabbed the feather-beds round and
        round,
    And the curtains they spared na' to
        tear them.

" It 's weel for me," said the wylie gude-
        wife,
    " That the Duke maun answer your
        breaking."
They gaed as they cam, and left a' things
        undone,
    And the young man was busy baking.

This rare little ballad is very musical through-
out, and deserves to find a place in the wallet
of our national vocalists.   It could be sung, I
fancy, to the tune of " Barbara Allen," though
of course in a livelier key.

THE HEIR OF LINNE.

The most dramatic of the ancient ballads
perhaps is the one that recounts the vicissi-
tudes of the Heir of Linne.   It is a tale of
unheroic life, in which not a word is said
about love or war, adventurous exploit or
supernatural agency, and yet it is replete with

interest, and related in an engaging style. A "ranting, roving," reckless young fellow was the said heir. Spending the day with merry cheer, devoting the night to drinking and gambling, his monetary resources became rapidly exhausted, and he was placed under the necessity of "selling his lands so broad, his house and lands, and all his rent." Even as Gilbert Glossan managed, with successful "might," to get hold of the Ellangowan estate that was "Bertram's right," so John o' the Scales, steward of the prodigal's deceased father, an unscrupulous money-grub, contrived to become Laird of Linne for a sum that did not represent more than a tithe of its value. Of all the extensive landed inheritance so-called, nothing was left to the thriftless loon "but a poor and lanesome lodge, that stood far off in a lanely glen"; and probably that too he would have parted with, had not his father, before dying, adjured him to retain it as a last friendly resource—

" My son, when I am gone," said he,
   " Then thou wilt spend thy land so broad,
And thou wilt spend thy gold so free ;
   But swear to me upon the rood,
That lanesome lodge thou 'll never spend ;
   For when all the world doth frown on thee,
There thou shalt find a faithful friend."

No longer a landed gentleman, "his bonnet stuck high upon his bree," he sank deep, deep in the mire of debasement. "Let's drink and rant and merry make," said he to the roystering blades who stood by him till his replenished money-bags were as empty of cash as Burns' "poor pouches" when the poet complained that the "meikle deil" had slipped into them to dance a reel. "The cock micht craw, and the day micht daw," ten times over, but they would still drink heroically "the barley bree." The rapid disappearance, pound after pound, of the red gold placed at his disposal by the sale of Linne, might warn the lord of the revels that the last coin of it would soon take the wings of the morning, and then grim ruin would stare him in the face; but he and his cronies continued their carousals till, in very deed—

> " Never a penny was left in his purse.
> Never a penny left but three;
> The tane was brass, the tither was lead,
> And the tither it was white monie."

To add to the mortification of the wastrel, his fair-weather companions disappeared along with his money. Though they forsook his society, he flattered himself into the belief that in his hour of need they would prove to be friends indeed, thus revealing the extreme

simplicity, not to say stupidity, of his own
character.

> " Many a trusty friend have I,
>   And why should I feel dool or care?
> I 'll borrow of them all by turns,
>   So need I not be ever bare."

> But one, I wiss, was not at home ;
>   Another had paid his gold away ;
> Another called him thriftless loon,
>   And sharply bade him mend his way.

" Well-a-way ! well-a-way ! and wae is me !"
sighed the spendthrift, as he encountered
these repulses. Continuing his doleful solilo-
quy, he declared that he could not work, that
he would not steal, that for him to beg his
bread from door to door would be a burning
shame. Then, as he could not want, off he
hied, half-despairing, to the mysterious " lane-
some lodge," to see if, peradventure, " a trusty
friend " would turn up there, as his father had
foretold. A miserable crib of a place was this
hermitage of the glen.

> He lookéd up, he lookéd down,
>   In hope some comfort for to win ;
> But bare and lothly were the walls :
> " Here 's sorry cheer," quoth the Heir of
>   Linne.

> The little window, dim and dark,
>   Was hung with ivy, brier, and yew;
> No shimmering sun here ever shone;
>   No halesome breeze here ever blew.

No cheerful hearth, no welcome bed, not an article of plenishing "mot he spye"; but, horrible to look at, a rope with a running noose hung dangling from the roof.

> And over it, in broad letters,
>   These words were written sae plain to see:
> " Ah! graceless, hast thou spent thy all,
>   And brought thyself to penurie?

> " All this my boding mind misgave,
>   I therefore left this trusty friend;
> Now let it shield thy foul disgrace,
>   And all thy shame and sorrow end."

Was ever poor wretch placed in a sorrier plight? A prey to dark despair, rendered doubly acute by the goadings of remorse, his heart was ready to burst "with guilt and sorrow, sin and shame"; and seeing no flicker of hope left, he bade the halter "right welcome" as a means of bringing him release from all his troubles. When this dismal crisis has been reached, the author of the ballad produces a powerful piece of stage effect, as if he had been composing a sensational melo-drama for modern playgoers. No sooner had the weight of the prodigal tested the strength of the "hempen gravat," and of the roof in which it was fixed, than

Lo! the ceiling burst in twain,
    And to the ground came tumbling he.

Astonished lay the Heir of Linne; and he was mightily comforted, as well as surprised, by finding a scrap of paper lying near him, and in it a suggestive key of gold. He rises, reads the billet, and, obeying the instructions it gives, seeks for a hole in the wall, which, when found, disclosed three chests in "fere"; and these having been unlocked, their hoarded treasures meet his ravished eye.

Two were full of the beaten gold,
    The third was full of white monie;
And over them in broad letters,
    These words were written sae plain to see:

" Once more, my son, I set thee clear,
    Amend thy life and follies past;
For, but amend thee of thy life,
    That rope must be the end at last."

" So let it be," said the Heir of Linne, " if I amend not"; but he took oath that the rede or counsel thus singularly supplied should guide him to the end. No longer a silly simpleton or a regardless sot, he has, though somewhat late in the day, learned wisdom in the school of experience, and nourishes the noble ambition of becoming once more the owner of his ancestral halls. That he may have a chance of bringing about this result, he lays a trap for the sordid man of the Scales. Shabbily attired, he presented himself at the house of that worthy, and prayed for the loan of forty pence, as he was in sore distress. John did not beat about the bush, but at once ordered the suppliant to be gone, swearing at the same time that he would not lend a single plack to such "a thriftless loon." Still keeping up the farce, the tatterdemalion petitioner applied most courteously to John's partner, Joan—

> " Madam, some awmous on me bestow,
>   I pray, for sweet Saint Charitie."

Her answer showed that the husband and wife were a well-matched pair—

> " Away, away, thou thriftless loon,
>   I swear thou gettest no alms of me ;
> For if we were to hang any losel here,
>   The first we wod begin with thee."

One of several lords who were birling at the social board with John, having heard the colloquy, tells the Heir of Linne, as he had been a rare good fellow in happier times, he would lend him forty pence, "and other forty if need there be." Then addressing the host on behalf of the Heir, he said—

" And ever I pray thee, John o' the Scales,
  To let him sit in thy companie,
For well I wot thou hadst his land,
  And a good bargain it was to thee."

This unlooked-for intercession was rendering his old friend greater service than he dreamed of by unwittingly furthering the scheme which was rapidly ripening to a successful issue.   Filled with indignation that may have been genuine, but could not have been virtuous, " up bespak him John o' the Scales," and declared solemnly that if he did not lose by that bargain might the curse of Christ rest upon his head—

" And here I proffer thee, Heir of Linne,
  Before these lords so fair and free,
Thou shalt have it back again better cheap
  By a hundred merks than I had it of thee."

This declaration prepared the way for a *dénouement* that surprised all present except the man who had brought it so craftily about.

"I draw you to record, lords," he said,
　　With that he cast him a God's pennie ;
"Now, by my fay," said the Heir of Linne,
　　"And here, good John, is thy monie."

And he pulled forth the bags of gold,
　　And laid them down upon the board ;
All woebegone was John o' the Scales,
　　So shent he could say never a word.

He told him forth the good red gold,
　　He told it forth with meikle din :
"The gold is thine, the land is mine,
　　And now I 'm again the Lord of Linne."

Giving forty pounds to the friend who had
offered to lend him forty pence, he took his
departure, while the matron of the house
bewailed her change of fate :

"Now, well-a-day," quoth Joan o' the Scales,
　　"Now, well-a-way, and woe is my life ;
Yesterday I was Lady of Linne,
　　Now I am but John o' the Scales his wife."

"Now, fare thee well," said the Heir of Linne,
　　"Farewell, good John o' the Scales," said he,
"When next I want to sell my lands,
　　Good John o' the Scales, I 'll come to thee."

KATHERINE JANFARIE.

When musing over this fine old ballad Sir Walter Scott was inspired to write his charming master-piece, " Young Lochinvar."   How much the great modern minstrel was indebted to his gifted but unknown predecessor may be seen from an analysis of the original ditty. In the latter case Lord Lochinvar does not figure as the triumphant wooer of the heroine, but as the man who comes off second-best. Crossing over the English Border to wed the lovely Katie, he courts the damsel at second hand.

> He told her father, he told her mother,
> And a' the lave o' her kin ;
> But he told na the bonnie May hersel'
> Till on her wedding e'en.

The lady had another sweetheart, one of the right kind, who prosecuted personally his own suit, and that with entire success.   This was Lord Lauderdale, who belonged, like herself, to the Scottish side of the Border.

> He told na her father, he told na her mother,
> And he told na ane o' her kin ;
> But he whispered the bonnie lassie hersel',
> And did her favour win.

"Come and see"; such was the laconic message he received from Katherine. To him it bore a world of meaning. He understood from it that his presence was urgently needed at her father's house on the day of her nuptials, and that she desired him to act the part of bridegroom in lieu of the English Lord. Lauderdale "sent word back again, 'Weel answered should she be.'" Accordingly he set out with four-and-twenty armed followers, and, halting them on the lee, he went by himself "to the wedding-house, to see what he could see."

But when he cam to the wedding-house,
　　He heard the music sound ;
And four-and-twenty belted knights
　　Sate at a table round.

He, being a nobleman of high renown, the guests rose up to bid him welcome, and entreated him to sit down with them and make himself at home. Nothing loth, Lauderdale complied, taking his share of "the good red wine" which "in silver cups did flow," the bride drinking to him, and exchanging glances with him so openly as to cause a commotion among the guests, and

　　Some began to whisper words,
　　　And some began to frown.

At the parallel stage in Sir Walter Scott's poem, the father of the bride, laying his hand on his sword, interrogates the intruder, " O come ye in peace here, or come ye in war, or to dance at our bridal ?" Language to the same effect is used by the bridegroom when addressing Lauderdale—

> " O come ye here for sport?" he said,
>   " Or come ye here for play ?
> Or come ye for our bonnie bride,
>   On this her wedding day ?"

> " I come na here for sport," he said,
>   " Nor come I here for play ;
> But for ae word o' your bonnie bride,
>   And then I 'll ride my way."

" He took her soft hand ere her mother could bar," he stepped aside with her for a moment, and the crisis they had arranged for came.

> They set her maidens her behind,
>   To hear what they would say ;
> The first word that he spake to her,
>   She lightly answered " Nay."
> The next word that he spake to her
>   Was " Mount, and come away."

If the lady, as reported, actually said " Nay," it could not have been by way of repulse ; for

with right good-will she acted in compliance
with his second invitation :

> He 's taen her by the milk-white hand,
>   And by the grass-green sleeve,
> He 's mounted her hie behind himsel',
>   At her kinsmen speered nae leave.

There was " racing and chasing," not on
" Canobie Lee," but in Caddondale, and, un-
happily, much hard fighting too, between the
followers of Lauderdale, who opportunely
appeared to protect the runaway pair, and
those of Lochinvar, by whom they were over-
taken.

> It 's up and owre the Caddon bank,
>   And down by Caddon brae ;
> The blood ran red on Caddon side
>   Before they wan away.

When the sanguinary strife was over, Lauder-
dale, in half regretful terms, congratulated his
Katherine on their escape—

> " My blessing on your heart, sweet thing !
>   Wae to your wilfu' will,
> There 's many a gallant gentleman
>   Whase blude ye have garr'd to spill."

The moral of the tale is thus set forth by the minstrel:

> Now all you lords of fair England,
>   That are in England born,
> Come never here to seek a wife,
>   For fear ye get the scorn.
>
> They 'll haik ye up and settle ye bye,
>   Till on your wedding day,
> Then gie you frogs instead of fish,
>   And play ye foul, foul play.

BURD HELEN.

The strength of woman's love, as we have already seen, has received lavish illustration from the old minstrels. It is strikingly manifested by Burd Helen, the heroine of our next legend. Lord John, her lover, was about to proceed home to the Highlands, and she, fearing he would never come back, prayed to be allowed to follow him in any way, or in any character, if it were only as a little foot-page. Lord John, who appears to have been a churlish fellow, with little nobility about him, save his title, points out the perils she would have to meet, and the difficulties she would have to overcome. But she heeded not his remonstrances, and away they set, he, shame to him, on milk-white steed, and she in man's attire—her luxuriant yellow locks remorselessly shorn away—running by his side.

> Lord John he rade, Burd Helen ran,
>   A livelong simmer day,
> Until they came to Clyde's water,
>   Was filled frae bank till brae.

The base-hearted knight, all unworthy of such devotedness, erroneously supposed that he would now get rid of his companion—

> "See'st thou yon water, Helen," said he,
>   " That flows from bank to brim ?"
> " I trust to God, Lord John," she said,
>   " You ne'er will see me swim."

> But he was ne'er sae lack a knight
>   As aince wad bid her ride,
> Nor did he sae much as reach his hand.
>   To help her owre the tide.

The first step took her to the knee; the second wetted her golden girdle; the third brought the water to her neck, till, the minstrel tells us, the child in her womb quaked for cold—

> And when she came to the other side
>   She sat down on a stane,
> Says : "Them that made me help me noo,
>   For I am far frae hame."

A most affecting picture. The weary, wae-fu' woman, barely escaped from drowning, dripping with wet, and fit to die of exhaustion and disappointment, in a strange country, the only one she knows being the hard-hearted man who has brought her to shame and the gates of death, and who has not a word of consolation or drop of pity to give her. She appeals to him once more, the light of love still shedding its rays on the dial of hope—

> " O, tell me this now, good Lord John,
>   In pity tell to me,
> How far is it to your lodging,
>   Where we this nicht maun be ? "

His answer was the bitterest that his bad heart could devise—

> " Oh, dinna you see yon castle, Helen,
>   Stands on yon sunny lea ?
> There ye'se get ane o' my mother's men,
>   Ye'se get nae mair o' me."

Burd Helen did not die despairingly from the stroke of these spoken daggers; she did not even answer reproachfully. In her heart love's overpowering emotion swallowed up all other sentiments and overcame even bodily weakness. She resolved, by an unprecedented display of patience and devotedness, to melt the flintiness of her lord's bosom, and become his honoured wedded wife—at least that she would not lose hope of becoming so as long as she was in life, and permitted to remain near his presence. She was determined, she said, at all events, come weal come woe, to love but him alone. The magnificent reception given to Lord John is next described by the balladist; but though there is a bevy of comely dames attendant upon him, Burd Helen in her menial occupation outshines them all—

> Four-and-twenty gay ladies
> Led him through bower and ha',
> But the fairest lady that was there
> Led his horse to the sta'.

We find her next set down in the kitchen to supper; but the supposed page, as may readily be conceived, has no heart for meat or drink, though pressed to partake of both by the servants:

> " O eat and drink, my bonnie boy,
> The white bread and the beer."
> " The never a bit can I eat or drink,
> My heart 's sae fu' o' fear."

> " O eat and drink, my bonnie boy,
> The white bread and the wine."
> " O the never a bit can I eat or drink,
> My heart 's sae fu' o' pine."

But Lord John's mother, being "a skeely" woman, expresses to him some doubts as to the sex of his attendant; and he, as if to allay her suspicion on this point, bids the bonnie boy hasten to the stable and give his horse corn and hay. When there, all unaided, Burd Helen brings forth a son. I must refer the reader to the ballad itself that he may see with what wonderful delicacy and tenderness all this is described. The narrative closes in the best style for a love tale, with a marriage. It transpires that the ignoble lord's repudiation of his sweetheart was chiefly caused by an unfounded fear that she would be unacceptable to his relatives, and that on learning the contrary, when the crisis was at its height, he resolved to act an honourable part to the mother of his child. But I must quote the concluding verses, as they bring out in still fuller relief the self-denial of Burd Helen, than whom no sweeter creation is to be found in all the realm of poetry, ancient or modern. During deep midnight, strange sounds reached the chamber in which Lord John's mother lay, those of a woman "maening" heavily, "a bairnie greeting sair;" "Win up, win up, my son," she said, "gae see how a' does fare;" and he, at her instance, repaired to the stable, which he found locked inside—

He hit the door then wi' his fit,
  Sae did he wi' his knee,
Till planks o' deal and locks o' airn
  To flinders he garr'd flee.

"An askin', an askin', Lord John," she says,
  "An askin' ye 'll grant me,
The meanest maid about your house
  To bring a drink to me.

" An askin', an askin', my dear Lord John,
  An askin' ye 'll grant me,
The meanest bower in a' your tower
  For thy young son and me."

" I grant, I grant your askin', Helen,
  A' that and mair frae me,
The very best bower in a' my tower
  For my young son and thee.

" O have thou comfort, fair Helen,
  Be of good cheer, I pray,
And your bridal and your kirking baith
  Shall stand upon ae day."

And he has ta'en her, Burd Helen,
  And rowed her in the silk ;
And he has ta'en his ain young son,
  And washed him in the milk.

And there was ne'er a gayer bridegroom,
  Nor yet a blither bride,
As they, Lord John and Lady Helen,
  Neist day to kirk did ride.

YOUNG BEKIE.

To the ballads already noticed in which a
marriage with the wrong lady or gentleman is
foreclosed at the eleventh hour, I have to add
another, the hero being young Bekie, a brave
Scottish knight, who obtains service at the
Court of France ; the heroine the French King's
fair daughter, Burd Isbel. They, of course,
became enamoured of each other. As Bekie
had no royal blood in his veins, he was thrown
into prison by the King's orders for his auda-
city in making love to the Princess. Listening
wistfully at the prison gate, Isbel heard her
lover lamenting his fate, and breathing a
prayer for deliverance—

"O gin a lady wad borrow me,
  At her stirrup I wad run ;
Or gin a widow wad borrow me,
  I wad swear to be her son.

"O gin a virgin wad borrow me,
  I wad wed her wi' a ring ;
I 'd gie her ha's, I 'd gie her bowers,
  The bonnie towers o' Linne."

Resolved on securing for husband the man who had already given her his heart, the devoted lady stole barefoot but and ben, so that her father might not be disturbed by her movements, and, seizing the keys of the dungeon, she speedily obtained an entrance, glad to see the captive once more, but shocked to find him in a truly wretched plight.

> " Wow but her heart was sair,
>   For the mice but and the bauld rattens
> Had eaten his yellow hair."

His face, long innocent of a razor, presented a lugubrious aspect, but, mindful of "small mercies," not less than of high heroic services—

> She 's gotten him a shaver for his beard,
>   A comber till his hair ;
> Five hundred pounds in his pocket,
>   To spend and no to spare.

With a "steed gude at need," royally saddled, and " a leash of hounds of ae litter," she filled up to overflowing the cup of her bounty. Delighted with his escape, especially as it had been brought about by the fair captor of his heart, he, before parting, joined in a solemn vow with her—

> That or three years were come and gane,
>   Weel married they should be.

Ungrateful, faithless, perjured knight of Linne! Before a twelvemonth had elapsed the alternative had been placed before him by his father that he must either marry a certain duke's daughter or lose his inheritance. With a sigh for Burd Isbel, he gave her up; and to please his cruel parent, and secure his own worldly interests, consented to wed a lady for whom he cared little or nothing. While the protracted festivities, which in these old times preceded the marriage ceremony, were going on, the French King's daughter was apprised of her lover's perfidy by a supernatural visitant—our old friend the Billy Blin. Waking her up from sleep, he appalled her with the statement that on that very day Bekie's wedding was taking place, and like the dear, good Brownie that he was, he laid before her a plan for the assertion of her own claims to be Bekie's bride, since she had become betrothed as his wife a year ago by solemn vow. So beautiful is the poetry in which Billy unfolds his scheme that I must give it entire, asking the reader to take special notice of the superb sumptuary appointments with which the narrative is rendered rich and sparkling.

"Haste and away," cried the benevolent Brownie—

" Ye'll do ye to your mother's bower,
　　As fast as ye can gang ;
And ye'll tak twa o' your mother's Maries,
　　To haud you unthocht lang.

" Ye'll dress yourself in the red scarlet,
　　The Maries in daintie green ;
And ye'll put girdles about your middle,
　　Wad buy an earldom.

" Syne ye'll gae doun by yon seaside,
　　And doun by yon sea-strand ;
And bonnie will be the Hollans boats
　　Come rowin' to your hand.

" Ye'll set your milk-white foot on board,
　　Cry, ' Hail, ye Domine ! '
And I will be the steerer o 't,
　　To row you o'er the sea."

No sooner had the Princess and her maidens
reached the seaside than the Dutch vessel
that was to carry them to Scotland came
" rowin' till their hand " as if endowed with
consciousness, " walking the waters as a thing
of life." Stepping on board, she greeted its
crew in the Lord's name, and then off it sailed,
the Billy Blin, according to his promise,
directing its course. How the Brownie looked
when so engaged remains unrecorded, but it

may be assumed that he wore a less eerie aspect than his famous Galloway brother, the typical Caledonian Brownie, when he appeared at Blednock farmhouse to tender his services. So uncanny did he seem that

The black dog growling covered his tail,
The lassie swarfed, let fa' the pail,
Rob's lingle brak as he men't the flail,
　At the sicht o' Aikendrum.

His matted head on his breast did rest,
A lang blue beard wan'ered doun like a vest,
And the glare o' his e'e hath nae bard ex-
　　pressed,
　Nor the skimes o' Aikendrum.

At all events, if "handsome is that handsome does," the Billy of our tale must have been no uncomely object. After getting his passengers safely landed, he drops from the scene, and is visible no more. Rapidity of movement on the part of the Princess was indispensable when all was at stake, and might have been ruined by ever so little delay. The porter at Bekie's gate having been won over by a gift of three merks, he, on bended knee, thus announced the fair visitors to his master—

" I have been porter at your yetts
    This thirty years and three,
But there are three ladies at them noo
    Their like I did never see.

" There 's ane o' them drest in red scarlet,
    And twa in dainty green ;
And they hae girdles about their middles,
    Wad buy an earldom."

But the Duke's daughter was gorgeously
apparelled too, and, naturally enough, did not
like to be looked upon as second-best on this
her wedding-day—

Then out and spak the burdly bride,
    Was a' gowd to the chin :
" If they be fine without," she says,
    " We'se be as fine within."

Had it been a mere question of dress that
was at issue, the bridegroom would probably
have been well content with the lady, so
buxom and so braw, who had given him her
hand ; but he felt that the fair visitor in red
scarlet could be none other than the lady
whom, even if she had been attired in rags, he
would have valued more than any other of her
sex. The reader has already anticipated the
result. What could the young man, who was
not of a high moral type, do, under the be-

wildering circumstances that had arisen, but
drop a tear or two, as he did, then hurry down
stairs, and, finding his presentiment cor-
rect, take Burd Isbel in his arms and " kiss
her tenderlie." With words of reproach that
breathed more of sorrow than of anger, the
noble-minded maiden thus addressed her
fickle lover—

> " O hae ye forgotten now, young Bekie,
>   The vow ye made to me,
> When I took ye out o' prison strang,
>   When ye was condemned to dee ? "

> " I gae you a steed was gude at need,
>   And a saddle o' royal bane ;
> A leash o' hounds o' ae litter,
>   And Hector called ane."

By this time an audience had assembled
that included the ill-used bride, her disgusted
papa, several of the wedding-guests, and the
good dog Hector, who manifested a sym-
pathetic interest in the speaker's statement,
and bore witness to its truthfulness—

> It was weel kent what the lady said,
>   That it was nae a lee ;
> For at the first word the lady spak,
>   The hound fell at her knee.

Turning to the Duke, young Bekie said—

" Tak hame, tak hame, your daughter dear,
    A blessing gang her wi' ;
For I maun marry my Burd Isbel,
    That 's come o'er the sea to me."

In this happy way terminated the wonderful adventures of Young Bekie. With a good grace the old nobleman submitted to the inevitable, making, however, a sarcastic retort—

" Is this the custom o' your house,
    Or the fashion o' your lan',
To marry a maid in a May morning,
    Send her back a maid at e'en ? "

HYNDE HORN.

Of the ballad so called there are several versions. One of them opens thus—

Near Edinburgh was a young child born,
    With a hey lillelu and a how lo lan ;
And his name it was the young Hynde
      Horn,
    And the birk and the brume bloom
      bonnie.

Seven lang years he served the King,
  With a hey lillelu and a how lo lan ;
And it 's a' for the sake of his dochter
    Jean,
  And the birk and the brume bloom
    bonnie.

These alternately repeated lines are continued throughout, giving melody to the ballad when sung ; but, as they rather injure its effect when read, I follow a copy from which they are omitted. The young Princess, fascinated with his manner, gave him for his fee what he valued vastly more than money wages ; and her father, learning how she had disposed of her heart, fell into a passion of rage, and banished the aspiring lover to a far land over the sea. Hynde himself is made to say before parting that he exchanged tokens with his sweetheart, he giving her a silver wand adorned with "three singing lavrocks," she giving him a talisman in the form of " a gay gold ring set with diamonds," and saying, ominously—

  " As lang as that ring keeps its hue,
  You 'll ken I am a lover true ;
  But when your ring turns pale and wan,
  Ye may ken I love another man."

The lady's foreboding of her own faithlessness

proved to be only too well founded. Pressed by her imperious father, I presume, the fickle maiden promised to reward another suitor with her hand, though Hynde Horn still occupied the foremost place in her heart. As for him, poor fellow, he had a weary lot of it, for "a year and a day," as a love-sick wanderer in a foreign country; but the magic ring he wore still sparkled with a radiance that was like the light of hope and consolation to his afflicted mind. Suddenly the sheen of the diamonds disappeared, leaving his future shrouded in gloom. Yet he did not despair. With characteristic courage and wisdom he resolved to return home and ascertain for himself how matters really stood. Possibly, he thought, my lady-love is still honest and faithful, and it is only this mischievous ring that is playing me false.

He 's left the seas and come to the lan',
And the first he met was an auld beggar man.

Accosting the gaberlunzie, he learned from him the doleful news that a wedding was going on at the palace, and that the bride was none other than his own betrothed. As in the case of Wallace with another "silly auld beggar" on a memorable occasion, Hynde Horn changed outer garments with the ancient carle, and off he set for the scene of the

revels to act his new part as a pleader for
charity. This he did to the life, having taken
a lesson from the genuine beggar before leav-
ing him.

> As he gaed up into the hill,
> His pike-staff he did bend him till ;
> And when he cam to the King's yett,
> He bided till they were at dinner set.

> He asked, for the sake o' Peter and Poule,
> An awmous for the beggar's cowl ;
> But awmous took he nane beside,
> Till he gat it frae the bonnie bride.

Though in these old days " the King's cauf"
was said to be better than other folk's corn,
a personal intercourse was kept up between
royalty and poverty that is rarely exemplified
in modern times. The King's daughter, in
this instance, did not deem it below her dignity
to leave the wedding-guests for the purpose of
conferring a favour on one whom she believed
to be a poverty-stricken traveller. Truly a
pleasant picture is set before us by the
balladist when he tells us how

> The bride cam tripping doun the stair,
> Wi' the kaims o' gowd intill her hair ;
> A cup o' red wine in her han',
> And that she gied to the beggar man.

Now came the chance which her disguised lover had plotted for all along. Ominous of evil had the ring been to him which he still wore. Might he not, by conjuring with it, make it operate as a minister for good? Drinking off the wine, he dropped the ring into the empty chalice, and anxiously waited for the issue. Taking up the tell-tale token, Lady Jean, trembling all over, asked—

> " O gat ye this by sea or by land,
> Or gat ye it frae a dead man's hand ? "

As music to her ear, and bringing rapture to her heart, came the reply in a voice which she recognised at once :

> " I gat it not by sea or by land,
> Nor gat it I on a dead man's hand ;
> But I gat it at my wooing gay,
> And I gie it to you on your wedding-day."

My own Hynde Horn, reduced to poverty, a prey to distress, but still the possessor of my affections, let me cast in my lot with thine !

> " I 'll tak the gowd kaims frae my head,
> I 'll follow thee and beg my bread ;
> I 'll tak the red gowd frae my hair,
> And follow thee for evermair ! "

At this critical stage we hear nothing about

the King or the deserted bridegroom. Sitting
upstairs, birling the flowing cup at the festive
board, they probably did not know till too late
that nuptials there could be none, seeing
the bride had fled to return no more. Fled,
not in the company of a gangrel loon wearing
a tattered cloak, according to the gossip of the
neighbourhood, but with a gentle cavalier who
had the best title to her, because to him she
had pledged her virgin troth. Rendered
dearer to him than ever by her resolution to
sacrifice position and wealth for his sake, he
felt overjoyed and thankful in being able to
assure her that he was still rich enough to
make her "lady of many a toun," that she
must therefore still retain the gowd kaims
for the ornamentation of her head-gear, even
as he himself was daintily attired; to prove
which,

Doon he loot his cloutit cloak fa',
    And the red gowd owre him a' shone out.

The bridegroom thought he had her wed,
    With a hey lillelu and a how lo lan;
But young Hynde Horn took her to bed,
    And the birk and the brume bloom
        bonnie.

THE GARDENER.

A young gardener who sighed for a partner, and thought the little spot he tilled would never be as Eden's bowers till he got one, tells a pretty tale of how he courted " a leal maiden, as jimp as a willow wand." The damsel happening to pass his way, he pays suit to her in a professional speech—

> " O lady, can ye fancy me,
>   And will ye be my bride ?
> Ye'se get a' the flowers in my garden
>   To be to you a weed.
>
> " The lily white shall be your smock,
>   It suits your body best ;
> A garland o' the gilly-flowers,
>   And a red rose on your breast.
>
> " Your goun shall be the sweetwilliam,
>   Your coat the camovine ;
> Your apron o' the ribbon grass
>   That grows sae tall and fine."

A very ingenious toilette this seems from a floral point of view; but the lady to whom it was tendered did not seem to care for it. She would, I fancy, have relished the gardener's wooing better if he had protested that there was not a flower in all creation that

could vie with her own personal charms;
neither was she won over when, to complete
the costume, he added a few other items—

> " Your shoon shall be the rosmarie,
>   Your garters o' woodbine,
> Your stockings o' the herb o' grace ;
>   Come, smile, sweetheart o' mine !

> " Your gloves shall be the marygold,
>   All glittering to your hand,
> Weel spotted wi' the blue blaewort
>   That grows amang corn land."

Like another proud Lady Marjorie, she
turned fiercely upon her suitor. His cold
symbolism indicated to her an absence of
the heart-warmth which plays such a magi-
cal part in the art of love-making ; but she
retorted with a bitterness that was scarcely
warranted—

> " Young man, and hae ye shaped me this
>   Amang the summer flowers ?
> Now I will shape a weed for you
>   Amang the winter showers.

> " The new-fa'en snaw to be your shirt,
>   It suits your body best ;
> Your head shall be wrapt wi' the eastern
>   wind,
>   And the cauld rain on your breast."

This curious conceit of a ballad is incomplete, and two verses are given by Herd which are supposed to have belonged to it, both of them very fine ; and as, slightly altered, they have been rendered classical by appearing in *Waverley*, they may be here fittingly introduced. When the hero of that romance was for the first time approaching Bradwardine Hall, he encountered half-witted Davie Gellatley, who, says Scott, " saluted the stranger by singing, with great earnestness, and not without some taste, a fragment of an old Scottish ditty—

" False love, and hast thou played me this
   In summer amang the flowers ?
I will repay thee back again
   In winter amang the showers.

" Unless again, again, my love,
   Unless you turn again ;
As you with other maidens rove,
   I 'll smile on other men."

PART SIXTH

MYTHOLOGICAL.

THOMAS THE RHYMER.

AMONG the laureates of Elf-land the first place must be assigned to Thomas of Ercildoune, or Thomas the Rhymer, the "day-starre" of Scottish poesy. He flourished in the golden days of Alexander III., and may possibly have given his patriarchal benedictions to the young Earl of Carrick, by whom, according to his prophecy, "The burn of bread" was to be made "run wi' red," in order that his country might be redeemed from English thraldom. True Thomas, as the poet is also called, is best remembered on account of his prophetic utterances. He wrote, too, a good deal about the fairy folks, as well as future events, which he was well fitted to do, not only because of his mystical cast of mind and fervid imagination, but because he in fact or fancy lived among them for several years. His visit to Elf-land and experiences there were described in a long poem that formed a prelude to his published book of prophecies, and they also form the theme of a brief popular ballad termed "True Thomas." The first of these productions is taken as the basis of our study, the second furnishing a few verses by way of illustration.

On a St. Andrew's Day, while the seer was making his moan by Huntly Banks, a fair apparition burst upon his enamoured gaze. This was the Fairy Queen, riding upon a palfrey, carrying a bugle-horn, and two leashes of hunting-dogs running at her horse's side ; but so lovely did she seem, and so gorgeously was she bedight, that he addressed her as the Queen of Heaven, though her accompaniments were less suggestive of the Blessed Mary of the Roman Calendar than the heathen goddess Diana. He said—

> " Yon is Mary most of micht,
>   That bare the Child that died for me ;
> But I speak with yon lady bricht,
>   I trow my heart will burst in three."

Having, it would seem, received some encouragement from his fair visitor, Thomas declared that he would follow her to the Eildon tree ; and in good sooth the pair proceeded thitherwards and entered upon a courtship under its shadow. He besought the lady to have compassion upon him—" lovely lady, reive on me,"—alleging that the pity for which he prayed would be in beautiful accordance with her sovereignty as the Virgin Mother—

> Then said that lady, mild of thought :
>   " Thomas, let such wordés be ;
> Queen of Heaven am I not,
>   For I took never so high degree."

Still keeping Thomas in the dark as to her identity, she simply informed him that she had left home on a hunting bout ; and thinking that she was on worldly pleasure bent, the enamoured poet daringly made love to her without more ado. He was warned by the Queen of two results that would flow from a compliance with his request—she would lose her beauty and he would lose his freedom. Thomas was already, however, the lady's helpless slave. Regardless of consequences, he replied—

> " Now, lovely lady, reive on me,
>   And I will evermore with thee dwell ;
> Here my troth I plight to thee,
>   Whether thou wonne in heaven or hell."

The scene of the Rhymer's temptation and fall is graphically described by the anonymous balladist—

> " Harp and carp, Thomas," she said,
>   " Harp and carp along with me ;
> But if you daur to kiss my lips,
>   Sure of your body I shall be."

But the lips were so enticing, and so much was their language belied by the tempting eloquence of her eyes, that he cast aside all restraint with the defiant exclamation—

> " Betyde me weal, betyde me woe,
>   That weird will never daunton me."

Suiting the action to the word, he rapturously saluted her rosy lips. Presto ! her beauty of person and her bravery of raiment vanished as if they had been waved over by the wand of some malignant enchanter.

Then said Thomas—

" Alace ! alace !
In faith this is a doleful sicht ;
How art thou faded thus in the face,
That shone before as the sun so bricht ! "

The unhappy Rhymer tells us that the lady
to whom he had sold himself bade him take
leave of all mundane things, and adapt him-
self to his new position as a subject of the
Fairy Queen. That then she led him "under-
neath a derne " of Eildon Hill, he beseeching
the veritable " Mary Mild " to forsake him
not, and devoutly recommending his soul to
Jesu. In a cavern dark as Erebus, and half-
filled with water, the poor captive pined for
three days, getting no sustenance all the time.
" Full woe is me !" he cried, " almost I die for
fault of food." As if the Queen had taken pity
upon him at last,

She led him into a fair herbaree,
    Where fruit was growing in great plentie ;
Pears and apples both ripe they were,
    The date, and also the damasce,

The fig, and also the wine-berry,
    The nightingales lying in their nest ;
The papinjays fast about 'gan flee,
    And throstles sung, would have no rest.

But these juicy-looking orchard products

might as well have been Dead Sea fruit to
him. He put forth his hand to pluck an apple,
but was warned by the tantalising lady to be-
ware lest it prove to him as baleful as the for-
bidden fruit of Eden's bowers. With words
of cheer, however, she bade him rest his head
upon her knee, and she would show him a
series of pictures strange. Thomas, having
right gladly complied with the Queen's request,
her panorama was unfolded. It is thus de-
scribed by the unknown ballad-writer—

  " O see ye na that braid, braid road,
   That stretches owre the lily leven ?
  That is the path of wickedness,
   Though some call it the road to heaven.

  " And see ye na yon narrow road,
   Sae thick beset wi' thorns and briers ?
  That is the path o' righteousness,
   Though after it but few inquires.

  " And see ye na yon narrow road,
   That winds about the ferny brae ?
  That is the way to fair Elf-land,
   Where you and I this nicht maun gae."

Still quoting from " True Thomas," I pre-
sent the following sketch of their travels,
which is at once so graphic and appalling—

O they rade on, and further on,
  And they waded through rivers abune
    the knee ;
And they saw neither the sun nor the
  mune,
  But they heard the roaring of a sea.

It was mirk, mirk nicht, there was nae
  stern-licht,
  And they waded through red blude to
    the knee ;
For a' the blude that's shed on the earth,
  Rins through the springs o' that coun-
    trie !

The rest of the adventures I shall take from
the prophet's own version. Pointing to a fair
castle, the Queen tells him that she resides in
it, as does also her husband, the King of the
country. This revelation about her wedded
partner must have been the reverse of pleas-
ant to Thomas ; and when she added that
hanging and drawing would be their doom if
the King " wist " of her infidelity to him, the
poet must, to say the least of it, have felt un-
easy. He was told to say nothing to any one
he might meet at the castle.

  " My lord is served at every mess
    With thirty knightés fair and free ;
  And I shall say, sitting at the dais,
    I took thy speech beyond the sea."

T

Before entering the royal presence she suddenly vanished; and while Thomas was "standing still as stane" she reappeared in a twinkling, charming and richly dressed as when he first beheld her. When he was ushered by the Queen into the castle hall, fair ladies fell at their feet; music of the finest, from harp, fiddle, lute, santry, rebeck, "and all manner of minstrelsy," saluted their ears; bright ladies dancing with handsome knights greeted their eyes; and the poet realised for the first time that he was now in Elfin-land. A happy period he had of it. So rapidly fled the golden hours that years seemed to him only days, and he was terribly chagrined when his fascinating patroness addressed him thus—

> " Go busk thee, Thomas, busk thee again,
>   For thou may'st here no longer be ;
> Hie thee fast, with might and main,
>   I shall thee bring to the Eildon tree."

Saddened at heart, Thomas prayed that he might be permitted to stay a while longer—the space of three days allotted to him, he said, being all too brief.

> " Forsooth, Thomas, I thee tell
>   Thou hast been here three year and more ;
> But longer here thou may'st not dwell,
>   The skill I will thee tell wherefore.

> "To-morrow of hell the foulé fiend
>   Among these folks shall choose his fee ;
> Thou art a fair man and a hende,
>   I trow full well he would choose thee."

With the custom here described of Elf-land paying tithe or teind to its feudal superior, the grim lord of Pandemonium, in the shape of a human subject, the poet must have been familiar. The idea that he should be made to illustrate it in his own experience must have been enough to drive him mad.

Was it real love for this son of earth that induced the Queen of Elf-land to secure his safety, or did she regulate her conduct by a desire to thwart the rival claim for his possession which she expected the fiend of hell would put forth? Her motive may have been a mixed one; yet she appears in a most amiable light, and as the possessor of a sensitive human conscience, when she tells True Thomas—

> " For all the gowd that ever may be
>   From heaven unto the worlde's end,
> Thou beest never betrayed by me,
>   Therefore with me I rede thee wende."

And the good Fairy Queen not only took the gifted poet safely back to Huntly Banks, but, if I understand properly her closing address, she endowed him with that spirit of prophecy to which he ever afterwards laid claim—

> " Fareweel, Thomas ; I wende my way,
>   I may no longer stand with thee."

But before she went he entreated her to leave with him some lasting memorial of their intercourse, to which she replied—

> " To harp and carp, wheresoever ye gone,
>   Thomas, take thee these with thee."

This offer of musical instruments might include those with which his ears were ravished in her enchanted castle ; but it was as a singer he sought to excel.

> " Harping," said he, " ken I nane,
>   For tongue is the chief of minstrelsie."

" If," she replied—

> " If thou wilt spell or talés tell,
>   Thomas, thou never shall make lee."

In other words, he was to be *True* Thomas, whether as a poet or prophet. Full surely he would comply with her farewell injunction—

> " Whithersoever thou go, to frith or fell, .
>   I pray thee speak never no ill of me."

TAMLANE.

We obtain some additional revelations of Elf-land from the rare old ballad of Tamlane. The fairies, it appears from it, were more desirous of getting young children than adults into their power; and if at any time they could capture an infant before it was " sained in christendie," that is to say, baptized, the prize was deemed particularly valuable, as in such a case the Church, with all its influence, was rarely able to rescue or redeem the captive. Even when the child had received the holy rite, it was a work of extreme difficulty to effect his emancipation, and establish him in a fraternity of ordinary flesh and blood. A modern poet who has very successfully imitated the old minstrels, relates in a felicitous style how Bonnie Kilmeny, after being carried off by the fairies, was permitted by them to return home for a brief space after a seven years' absence—

> With distant music soft and sweet,
> They lulled Kilmeny sound asleep ;
> And when she awakened she lay her lane,
> All happed with flowers in the green wood
> wane.

When seven long years had come and fled,
When grief was calm, and hope was dead,
When scarce was remembered Kilmeny's
    name,
Late, late in a gloamin' Kilmeny cam hame.

But this was a rare privilege, the general rule being for the Queen of Elf-land to retain hold of her human subjects till deprived of her influence over them by counteracting charms. How a fair damsel, by strong spells of disenchantment, and the dint of irresistible love, redeemed her bosom's lord, is well described by the ballad before us.

Sweet Janet, its heroine, foolishly persists in going to a favourite haunt of the fairies, though warned in the opening words—

O I forbid ye, maidens a',
    That wear gowd in your hair,
To come and gae by Carterhaugh,
    For young Tamlane is there.

Being a genuine daughter of mother Eve, her curiosity was piqued. She goes all alone to the perilous place, and there sure enough forgathers with the mysterious mannikin, and almost, as a matter of course, a love intrigue is the consequence. In a second interview she interrogates the stranger as to his antecedents, present position, and future prospects.

"The truth ye 'll tell to me, Tamlane,
  A word ye mauna lee ;
Gif e'er ye was in haly chapel,
  Or sained in christendie."

His answer opens up a nice bit of romance—

" The truth I 'll tell to thee, Janet,
  A word I winna lee ;
A knight me got, a lady me bore,
  As well as they did thee.

" Randolph, Earl Murray, was my sire,
  Dunbar, Earl March, was thine ;
We loved when we were children small,
  Which yet you well may mind.

" When I was a boy just turned of nine,
  My uncle sent for me,
To hunt, and hawk, and ride with him,
  And keep him companie.

" There came a wind out of the north,
  A sharp wind and a snell ;
And a dead sleep cam over me,
  And frae my horse I fell.

" The Queen o' Fairies keppit me,
  In yon green hill to dwell ;
And I 'm a fairy, lith and limb ;
  Fair lady, view me well."

So it seems the instinctive promptings of an old infantile attachment combined with feminine curiosity to lead Janet at first to Carterhaugh. Tamlane went on to tell her how happy he would be but for one tormenting idea. Once in every seven years Elf-land, as in the case of True Thomas, had to pay homage to the foul fiend by yielding up to him one of its human subjects, and—horrible thought!—he was likely to be selected as the offering this term, as he was exceedingly plump and fair of flesh, and that very day he might be sacrificed to Satan. Thereupon he thus exhorts the damsel—

> "This nicht is Halloween, Janet,
> The morn is Hallowday;
> And, gin ye dare your true love win,
> Ye hae nae time to stay.

> "The nicht it is gude Halloween,
> When fairy folks will ride;
> And they that wad their true love win,
> At Miles Cross they maun bide."

In answer to inquiries how she would be able to recognise him in the cavalcade, he said that he would ride a milk-white steed, and rank nearest the town, that post being allotted to him because he was a christened knight.

Then, the moment he approached, she was to
pull him from his horse, and hold him fast,
though his unearthly colleagues would turn
him first into an adder, then into a snake, then
into a fiery fagot, and last into a red-hot
bar of iron; but she was still to retain her
grasp, or he would be lost to her for ever.
This was not the whole of the trying and
terrible ordeal. After undergoing these meta-
morphoses, she was to dip him in a stand of
milk, and then in a stand of water, and
when the seeming bar of red-hot iron was
thus cooled down, it was to turn into a loath-
some swimming reptile, and then into a fish.

> " And, next, they 'll shape me in your arms,
>   A toad, but and an eel ;
> But haud me fast, let me not gang,
>   As you do love me weel."

To birds of the air was the next and closing
series of changes.

> " They 'll shape me in your arms, Janet,
>   A dove, but and a swan ;
> And, last, they 'll shape me in your arms,
>   A mother-naked man :
> Cast your green mantle over me—
>   I 'll be myself again."

It required no ordinary amount of courage

to carry out such injunctions. Night was the time when the dreaded fairy folk held their great annual saturnalia, and on this occasion the vault of heaven was uncheered by a single star.

> Gloomy, gloomy was the nicht,
>   And eerie was the way,
> As fair Janet, in her green mantle,
>   To Miles Cross she did gae.

There she stands "at the solemn hour when night and morning meet," while the north wind bears on its blast strange eldritch sounds enough to freeze her blood or drive her mad. Panoplied in the armour of love, she is proof against superstitious fear, and she feels a thrill of positive joy when the ringing of bridles announces that the mystic regiment is at hand. The fairy troopers ride up and pass—

> And first gaed by the black, black steed,
>   And then gaed by the brown ;
> But fast she gript the milk-white steed,
>   And pu'd the rider down ;

To the astonishment and mortification of his elfish companions—

> She pu'd him frae the milk-white steed,
>   And loot the bridle fa' ;
> And up there raise an eldritch cry—
>   " He 's won amang us a' !"

They exhausted their whole quiver of spells
with the view of unlocking her arms and re-
gaining the ravished knight, but in vain—

They shaped him in fair Janet's arms,
    An ask but and an adder;
She held him fast in every shape—
    To be her bairn's father.

They shaped him in her arms at last,
    A mother-naked man ;
She wrapt him in her green mantle,
    And sae her true love wan.

And I think the reader will agree with me
that she well merited such a triumph.   The
ballad closes with a characteristic speech from
the exasperated Fairy Queen :

Up then spoke the Queen o' Fairies
    Out o' a bush o' rye,
" She 's ta'en away the bonniest knight
    In a' my companie.

" But had I kenn'd, Tamlane," she says,
    " A lady wad borrowed thee,
I wad ta'en out thy twa gray een,
    Put in twa een o' tree.

" Had I but kenn'd, Tamlane," she says,
    " Before ye cam frae hame,
I wad ta'en out your heart o' flesh,
    Put in a heart o' stane.

" Had I but had the wit yestreen
    That I hae coft the day,
I 'd paid my kane seven times to hell
    Ere you 'd been won away."

ALISON GROSS.

There were good fairy queens as well as
spiteful, mischievous ones in the old mytho-
logy. The writer of our next ballad found
this to be the case in his own happy experi-
ence. An aged beldame, who had no natural
charms, but had the spells of a sorceress at
her command, became enamoured of our
minstrel-hero, and with many fair speeches
induced him to enter her bower. She seems
to have played the part of the venomous spider
in the nursery song, and he to have been
quite as verdantly simple as the poor fly which
it victimised. Though Alison Gross was " the
ugliest witch in the north countrie," he
allowed himself to be caught in her toils ;
and she, having got him fairly entrapped, made
love to him as if she had been a winsome
lady. She, he says—

Straiked my head, and she kamed my hair,
    And she set me doun saftly on her knee.

Next she sought to melt his still obdurate

heart by proffering him " mony braw things "
if he would only become " her leman sae
true "—

> She showed me a mantle o' red scarlet,
>   Wi' gowden flowers and fringes fine ;
> Says, " Gin ye will be my leman sae true,
>   This gudely gift it sall be thine."

The further stages of this one-sided court-
ship are vigorously described—

> " Awa, awa, ye ugly witch,
>   Haud far awa, and let me be ;
> I never will be your leman sae true,
>   And I wish I were oot o' your companie."

Our poet does not mince matters. The
wonder is, when Alison Gross was thus ad-
dressed, she did not at once make the man
who had despised her as a woman feel her
power as a witch.

> She neist brocht a sark o' the saftest silk,
>   Weel wrought wi' pearls about the band ;
> Says, " Gin ye will be my ain true love,
>   This gudely gift ye may command."

> She showed me a cup o' the gude red gowd,
>   Weel set wi' jewels sae fair to see ;
> Says, " Gin ye will be my leman sae true,
>   This gudely gift I will you gie."

As his reply was no less obdurate than before, it brought the parley to an end, and precipitated a crisis—

" Awa, awa, ye ugly witch,
  Haud far awa, and let me be ;
For I wadna ance kiss your ugly mouth,
  For a' the gifts that you could gie."

She's turned her richt and round about,
  And thrice she blew on a grass-green horn;
And she sware by the moon and the stars
    aboon,
  She'd gar me rue the day I was born.

Then out has she ta'en a silver wand,
  And she's turned her three times round
    and round ;
She muttered sic words that my strength it
    failed,
  And I fell doun senseless on the ground.

She turned me into an ugly worm,
  And gart me toddle about the tree ;
And aye, on ilka Saturday's nicht,
  Auld Alison Gross she cam to me.

Came to gloat over the humiliation of her victim? Not so. The ancient lady seemed to be herself more than bewitched by the " ugly worm," still seeing in it the dear object of her blighted affections. Yes, and she is represented as placing the " toddling " reptile upon her knee, and dressing its wee " headie wi' silver basin and silver kaim." But all without avail, the man in the worm protesting mentally that he would rather keep crawling among the grass than return her caresses. The picture is grotesque in the extreme. The ballad artist who drew it believed in its truthfulness, however, and so would the crowds before whom it was displayed. At the date of the tale, probably about two hundred and fifty years ago, the people of Scotland gave implicit credit to more marvellous feats in connection with witchcraft than those attributed to old Alison Gross. When at length the subject of her enchantments obtained deliverance from them, it was, as already hinted, through the benevolent intervention of the Queen of Elf-land, who accidentally discovered him when riding by with her court " last Halloween." This he makes known with dramatic effect in his closing stanza—

She took me up in her milk-white hand,
    And she straiked me three times owre her
      knee ;
She changed me again to my ain proper
      shape,
    And I nae mair need toddle about the tree.

PROUD LADY MARGARET.

Proud Lady Margaret broke the hearts of many suitors. Haughty and disdainful, she would not so much as vouchsafe them a glance of pity when, slaves to her beauty, they knelt despairingly at her feet. To "a stranger knight," who, on entering into her presence during a moonlight eve, declared he was dying for her sake, her answer was still the same—freezing and repellent—

> " If you should die for me, young man,
>   There 's few for you will mane ;
> For mony a better has died for me,
>   Whose graves are growing green."

There was, however, a mysterious something about the lady's new lover which arrested her attention. While pressing his plea, he affirmed that he was " a courteous," that is, a high-born " knight." " It may be so," said the damsel,

> " But I misdoubt ye sair ;
> I think you 're but a miller lad,
>   By the white clothes ye wear."

In this indirect way we learn that the visitor, like the Willie of a previous ballad, has come from the spirit world, and it is soon

made known that he is armed with a commis-
sion from Providence to rebuke Lady Margaret
for her pride, and to teach her humility by
lessons drawn from the noisome charnel-house.
As if the lady weened he had more than
mortal wit, she propounded a series of riddles,
with the intimation that unless he " read
them richt," he might just "stretch him out
and dee "—

" What is the fairest flower, tell me,
   That grows on muir or dale ?
And what is the bird, the bonnie bird,
   Sings next the nightingale ?
And what is the finest thing," she says,
   " That king or queen can wale ?"

" The primrose is the first flower
   That springs on muir or dale ;
The mavis is the sweetest bird
   Next to the nightingale ;
And yellow gowd 's the finest thing
   That king or queen can wale."

" But what is the little coin," she said,
   " Wad buy my castle bound ?
And what 's the little boat," she said,
   " Can sail the world all round ?"

" O hey, how mony small pennies
   Mak thrice three thousand pounds ?

U

> O hey, how mony salt fishes
>   Swim a' the saut sea round?"

It was to pride of intellect more than anything else that the lady's consuming arrogance was due. Finding herself fairly vanquished in this tournament of words, she said, with a meekness that was strange to her, and which gave a new grace to her beauty—

> "I think ye are my match—
>   My match, and something mair;
> Ye are the first that got the grant
>   Of love frae my father's heir."

Then the lady lets him see what a goodly dower she has, her besetting sin manifesting itself in her somewhat bragging display—

> "My father was lord o' nine castles,
>   My mother lady o' three;
> My father was lord o' nine castles,
>   And there's nane to heir but me:"

Adding pathetically, after a short pause—

> "Unless it be Willie, my ae brother—
>   But he's far ayont the sea."

Strange and startling is the response of her visitor—

> " If your father's lord o' nine castles,
>   Your mother lady o' three ;
> It's I am Willie, your ae brother,
>   Was far ayont the sea."

Strong sisterly love prompted Margaret's reply. Clinging to the belief that her long-lost brother, her "Wandering Willie," now returned, was still a being of flesh and blood, she declared, Ruth-like, that she was resolved to go with him whithersoever he went. He affirmed that, fond sister though Margaret was, she could not accompany him with her feet and hands "ill-washen," and her garments so coarse, though the robes she wore were, in a mundane sense, rich and fine. She must now have fully realised the cruel truth that it was with her brother's ghost she had been holding parley. Opening up the mystery by degrees, he went on to tell why he had paid her this extraordinary visit—

> " My body 's buried in Dumfermline,
>   Sae far ayont the sea ;
> But day nor nicht nae rest can I get,
>   A' for the pride o' thee."

Then follows a powerful homily—

> " Leave off your pride, Margaret," he says,
>   " Use it not ony mair ;

Or when ye come where I hae been,
   You will repent it sair.

" Cast off, cast off, sister," he says,
   " The gowd band frae your croun :
For if you gang where I hae been,
   You 'll wear it laigher doun.

" When you are in the gude kirk set,
   The gowd pins in your hair,
Ye tak mair delicht in your feckless dress
   Than in your morning prayer.

" And when ye walk in the kirkyard,
   And in your dress are seen,
There is nae lady that sees your face
   But wishes your grave were green."

Finally the affectionate and faithful monitor adjured Margaret that a seat in Pirie's chair, situated in the depth of the nether regions, would assuredly be hers unless she mended her ways forthwith—

Wi' that he vanished frae her sicht,
   In the twinkling of an eye ;
And naething mair the lady saw,
   But the gloomy clouds and sky.

CLERK SAUNDERS.

Whether looked at as a love tragedy or as a tale of superstitious folk-lore, Clerk Saunders is a deeply interesting ballad. It resembles several old ditties already passed under review, inasmuch as the hero is put to death when sleeping in the arms of his sweetheart, visits her afterwards to claim back his faith and troth, and is followed by her to the land of graves; but it has some special features of its own, one of these being that the suitor is in training for the priesthood, and therefore contemplating a single life, if not sworn to celibacy. As if ominous of coming disasters, a pathetic key-note is struck in the opening stanza—

> Clerk Saunders and May Margaret
>   Walked owre yon garden green;
> And sad and heavy was the love
>   That fell them twa between.

Margaret, pressed by him to surrender her charms to his illicit embrace, resolutely declines, telling him that they must be married first, as if there had been no legal impediment to their union; the lady adding warningly—

> " For in may come my seven bauld brothers,
>   Wi' torches burning bright ;
> They 'll say—' We hae but ae sister,
>   And behold she 's wi' a knight.' "

With a stroke of casuistry that does not seem very convincing to the modern eye, the impassioned Clerk destroys her scruples—

> " Then tak the sword from my scabbard,
>   And slowly lift the pin ;
> And you may swear, and save your aith,
>   You never let me in.

> " And tak a napkin in your hand,
>   And tie up baith your een :
> And you may swear, and save your aith,
>   You never let me in."

Full surely, as May Margaret had surmised, in came her brothers at the midnight hour, when she and her paramour were fast asleep. Six of them viewed the case with leniency, but the seventh—" an ill deid may he dee "— stepped forward, and, saying never a syllable,

> Striped his bright brown brand
> Through Saunders' fair bodie.

Clerk Saunders "started," and Margaret "turned into his arms as asleep she lay;" then, we are told,

Sad and silent was the nicht
    That was between thir twae.

The poor lady, though asleep, was sympa-
thetically affected by the treacherous murder
of her true love; and he was perforce silent,
under the speech-destroying spell of death,
"sleeping the sleep which knows no waking."

He lay still, and sleepit sound.
    Till the day began to daw;
And kindly to him she did say—
    "It is time, love, you were awa."

Even when the sun began to shine he made
no response to May Margaret's call, nor did
she realise the cause of his silence till

She looked atween her and the wa',
    And dull, dull were his een;
She turned the blankets to the foot,
    The sheets unto the wa',
And there, anent his bonnie heart,
    The bluidy wound she saw.

Just as she had begun to realise the full horror
of the situation, and was uttering a malediction
on her "fause brothers" who had brought it
about, her father entered to console her with
the promise of getting her "a higher match,"
but his words only added to her anguish.

> "Gae wed, gae wed your seven sons,
>   Ill wedded may they be,
> Sin they hae killed my ain true love,
>   For wedded I ne'er shall be."

True to her resolution, she remained single and sorrowful for "a twelvemonth and a day," after the lapse of which period we find her, while sitting in the bower that had been the scene of her sin and its terrific sequel, startled by a strange "knock and cry."

> "O are ye a thief or robber," she says,
>   "That comes to burn or break?
> Or are ye ony maisterfu' man
>   Is seeking of a maik?"

> "I am not ony thief," he says,
>   "Nor do I seek a maik;
> But I 'm Clerk Saunders, your ain love,
>   Come here with thee to speak.

> "I canna rest, Margaret," he says,
>   "In the grave, where I maun be,
> Till ye give me my faith and troth again,
>   I wot, true love, I gied thee."

Then follows a singular colloquy, which affords us some curious information about the spirit land as presented to the poetic eye of the old minstrels, and devoutly credited by their

countrymen. Why the ghostly visitor is so
bent on getting relieved from his vow is not
stated; but it may be inferred, I think, that
he would have looked upon it as irrevocable
had it been deemed proper and valid by the
canons of the Church, and had it involved no
trouble of conscience or bodily penance. As
if to identify the apparition, and put his
sincerity to the test, Margaret responded
thus—

> "Your faith and troth ye sall never get,
>   Nor our true love sall never twin,
> Until ye come within my bower,
>   And kiss me, cheek and chin."

Fearing that Margaret's request, if complied
with, would prove instantly fatal to her, he
declined it, and repeated his plea.

> " O cocks are crowing a merry midnight,
>   I wot the wild-fowls are boding day;
> Give me my faith and troth again,
>   And let me fare me on my way."

Margaret professed her conditional readiness
to grant him the release he prayed for.

> " Thy faith and troth ye sall never get,
>   Nor our true love sall never twin,
> Until ye tell what comes of women,
>   I wot, who die in strong traivelling."

This conundrum was, I fancy, designed to test the spirit's knowledge of the land from which he professed to come. Had he been puzzled by it, the scepticism which lurked in the lady's mind might have acquired new force, but he solved it to her satisfaction by saying—

"Their beds are made in the heavens high,
    Doun at the feet of our Good Lord's knee,
Weel set about wi' gillyflowers:
    I wot sweet company for to see.

"O cocks are crowing a merry midnight,
    I wot the wild-fowls are boding day;
The psalms of heaven will soon be sung,
    And I, ere now, shall be missed away."

Reluctantly, and with sad misgivings of heart, the lady cancelled all his obligations to her, and then, strange though it may seem, fell under his fascinating influence more than ever.

Then she has ta'en a crystal wand,
    And has stroken her troth thereon;
She has gien't him oot at the shot window,
    Wi' monie a sigh and heavy groan.

"I thank ye, Margaret; I thank ye, Margaret;
    And aye I thank ye heartilie;
Gin ever the dead cam for the quick,
    Be sure, Margaret, I 'm come for thee."

Obeying a summons that she felt to be irre-
sistible,

> Sae painfully she clam the wa',
>   She clam the wa' up after him,
> Hosen nor shoon upon her feet,
>   She hadna time to put them on.

As in the case of other apparitions already met
with, Clerk Saunders, who had been recount-
ing his exalted experiences as a spirit in
heaven, seems suddenly transformed into a
tenant of tombland, with all its dreary and
repellent accompaniments. Arrived at his
noisome, earthly resting-place, May Margaret,
such was the love she cherished for him, in-
sisted upon sharing his lowly bed.

> " Is there onie room at your head, Saunders?
>   Is there onie room at your feet?
> Or onie room at your side, Saunders,
>   Where fain fain I wad sleep?"

Clerk Saunders refused to sanction the self-
sacrifice which these words implied. She had
suffered more than enough for his sins already,
and he unselfishly exhorted her to cherish life
and hold herself free from all obligation to him.

> " There 's nae room at my head, Margaret,
>   There 's nae room at my feet ;
> My bed it is full lowly now :
>   Mang the hungry worms I sleep.

"Cauld mould is my covering now.
  But and my winding-sheet;
The dew it fa's nae sooner doun
  Than my resting-place is weet.

" But plait a wand o' the bonnie birk,
  And lay it on my breast;
And gae ye hame, May Margaret,
  And wish my saul gude rest.

" And fair Margaret, and rare Margaret,
  And Margaret o' veritie,
Gin e'er ye love another man,
  Ne'er love him as ye did me."

Then up and crew the milk-white cock,
  And up and crew the gray;
Her lover vanished in the air,
  And she gaed weeping away.

WILLIAM'S GHOST.

Our next ballad bears a strong resemblance
to Clerk Saunders, and is, like it, a fine
specimen of the ancient minstrelsy. Some of
the apparitions introduced by it seem at first
to carry their "mortal coil" with them, but
the opening verse of the tale before us states
in plain terms, "There cam' a ghost to Mar-
jorie's door." The uncanny visitor had to

tirl persistently at the pin before the lady made any response. "Is that my father Philip?" she at length asked, or "My brother John, or my true love Willie, from England new come hame?" "Your Willie it is," was the reply. Welcome news indeed was this to her. She was delighted to hear his voice again; the prospect of getting handsome presents from the long absent wanderer giving additional warmth to her greeting and welcome.

> "Hae ye brocht me ony scarlets fine?
>   Or ony new thing to wear?
> Or hae ye brocht me a pearlin' braid,
>   To snood up my gowden hair?"

Raiment for the dead he brings, but no such costume for the quick. But the precise situation was not understood by the lady, even when Willie's next words, uttered in sepulchral tones, fell upon her ear—

> "I havena brocht the scarlets fine,
>   Or pearlin' for your hair;
> I 've brocht ye but my winding-sheet,
>   And that you wadna wear."

Next the visitor plainly revealed the object he had in view. When still in the flesh he had, Lothario-like, trifled with the affections

of at least four maidens, including Marjorie.
He had sworn to make her his bride : because
he had not kept his solemn promise, made
upon oath, he could get no rest in his grave,
and he now prayed her to relieve him from
the remorseful burden of an unfulfilled vow—

> "Oh sweet Marjorie ! oh dear Marjorie !
>   For faith and charitie,
> Give me again the faith and troth
>   That I gave once to thee."

> "This I will not do," she said,
>   "Nor yet our true love twin,
> Till that you come within my bower,
>   And kiss me cheek and chin."

Knowing that if his lips touched hers " her
days would not be lang," he refuses, and
pressingly repeats his request—

> "The cocks are crawing, Marjorie,
>   The cocks are crawing again ;
> It's time the deid suld pairt frae the quick,
>   Marjorie, I must be gane."

> "O, Marjorie, dear Marjorie,
>   For faith and charitie,
> Give me my faith and troth again
>   That I gave once to thee !"

Even yet the bewildered damsel puts far from

her the idea that she is conversing with her
lover's ghost, and entreats him to be true to
her as the best means for securing his own
peace of mind—

> " Tak me to your ha' hoose, Willie,
>   And wed me wi' a ring."

Neither would she give him up when he
assured her once more that his house was a
" lanesome grave, afar out over yon lea," and
that it was only her Willie's spirit with which
she was holding converse. Like the Lizzie
Lindsay of another ancient lay, she " kiltet
her robes o' green satin a little below her
knee," as he glided off,

> And a' the livelong winter nicht
>   The deid corpse followed she.

Thus, in some mystic way unexplained, the
spirit assumed its fleshly garment during this
ghostly travel to the place of tombs.

> She followed him high, she followed him low,
>   Till she cam to yon kirkyard green ;
> And there the deep grave opened up,
>   And William he lay doun.

A supernatural assize ensues, in which the
poetic minstrel, by a stroke of fancy bordering

on the sublime, summons the spirits of three
young women and their infants to prove the
perfidy of Marjorie's lover.   Interrogating
him, as the prisoner at the bar of conscience,
in regard to the personality of the witnesses,
and the evidence they have to offer—

> "What three things are these," she said.
>   "That stand here at your heid?"
> "Oh! it's three maidens, Marjorie,
>   That I promised once to wed."

> "What three things are these," she said,
>   "That stand close at your side?"
> "Oh! it's three babies, Marjorie,
>   That these three maidens had."

The guilt of the trafficker in women's hearts
has been thoroughly proved by evidence and
his own confession; nothing is left now but
to pronounce judgment; and lo! a pack of
fiends lie near, ready and eager to carry it
into effect.

> "What three things are these," she said,
>   "That lie close at your feet?"

And Willie's answer is—

> "Oh! it's three hell-hounds, Marjorie
>   That's waitin' my soul to keep."

Devoted to Willie still, alike in death as in life, Marjorie freely forgives his faithlessness to her ; and, awed by the majesty and purity of her demeanour, the three furies slink away, leaving him unharmed. Well might Willie term her " Sweet Marjorie, and dear Marjorie," and the balladist might, without any undue poetic licence, have called his heroine divine, as she shrives him with the palmistry of Christian forgiveness, and gives him peace—

Then she's taen up her white, white hand,
    And struck him on the breist,
Saying, " Have thee again your faith and troth,
    And I wish your soul good rest."

YOUNG BENJIE.

A deadly quarrel between two lovers is the theme of our next tale, and it affords also a fresh illustration of the superstitious folk-lore to which our ancestors pinned their belief. Most devoted to each other were young Benjie and fair Marjorie. Both of them were high-spirited ; they had frequent differences, but they loved so " constantlie,"

    That aye the mair when they fell out,
      The sairer was their plea.

That is to say, the kiss of mutual forgiveness made the bond between them stronger than before ; till, alack! in an unhappy moment Benjie said or did something to Marjorie which "made her heart grow wae," and resolve to choose another lover. Probably the resolution was soon repented of, the thoughts of her heart still turning to Benjie, as the only swain for whom she cared. Oh! if he had only yielded a little, have compromised the quarrel with ever such a morsel of an apology for his offence, what a joy he would have conferred upon her, and from what awful guilt and fearful retribution he would himself have been saved! But he was "stout and proud-hearted," he brooded bitterly on the thought of his rejection by Marjorie, and in revengeful mood he went to her bower-door, scarcely needing the "wan moonlight" that shone around to guide him along the familiar way. To his entreaty, " Open, my true love, and let me in," she returned an evasive, if not an untruthful, answer. Her three brothers were in the house, she said, and his admission was impossible. That is a false statement, he replied, for as " I cam by the Lowden banks, they bade gude-e'en to me."

> " But fare ye weel, my ae fause love,
> 　That I have loved sae lang !
> It sets ye choose another love,
> 　And let young Benjie gang."

Thoroughly overcome by these words, all the proud obduracy that still remained in her heart melted away.

> Then Marjorie turned her round about,
> The tear blinding her e'e,—
> "I daurna, daurna let thee in,
> But I 'll come doun to thee."

> Then saft she smiled, and said to him,
> "O, what ill hae I dune?"

At that moment they were standing on the brink of a deep pool. Choice on the part of Benjie, not chance, fixed that perilous verge as their meeting-place. He embraced her with apparent fondness, and as if about to pour blessings on her head and plant kisses on her lips—Judas-like salutes they would have been had he given her any, as it was but the malice of murder aforethought that led the implacable villain to take the trustful Marjorie in his arms. The next moment the poor lady was struggling for sheer life in the gaping linn below. Stout of body she was, and "laith, laith to be dang"; but ere she reached the Lowden banks her strength gave way, her rosy cheek grew wan, and her spirit fled. The corpse was discovered by her three brothers, though they could scarcely identify it till evidence was supplied in the form of a honey-mark on her chin, which, having been seen by them, they could no longer doubt that the body was that of their dear sister.   They concluded also that she had experienced foul play, and began to ask,

> " O wha has killed our ae sister,
>   And how can he be found ? "

In the absence of living witnesses, they resolved to take the steps that were customary on such occasions, of making an appeal to the dead body.

> " The nicht it is our low lyke-wake,
>   The morn her burial day ;
> And we maun watch at mirk midnicht,
>   And hear what she will say."

> With doors ajar and candles licht,
>   And torches burning clear,
> The streikit corpse, till still midnicht,
>   They wake, but naething hear.

> About the middle o' the nicht,
>   The cocks began to craw ;
> And at the dead hour o' the nicht,
>   The corpse began to thraw.

This motion of the body induced the workers of the charm to proceed with their inquiry, as they knew that the spirit of the dead maiden

had re-entered its earthly tabernacle in order
to reveal her secret—

> " O whae has done this wrang, sister,
>   Or daured this deadly sin ?
> Whae was sae stout, and feared nae doubt,
>   As thraw ye owre the linn ? "

Then came the response—

> " Young Benjie was the first ae man
>   I laid my love upon ;
> He was sae stout and proud-hearted,
>   He threw me owre the linn."

Appealing to the spirit as both witness and
judge, the brethren now asked—

> " Shall we young Benjie head, sister ?
>   Shall we young Benjie hang ?
> Or shall we pyke out his twa grey e'en,
>   And punish him ere he gang ? "

One might have been tempted to suppose
that the punishment meted out by Marjorie
to the criminal would have been light, or
purely nominal because of their past relation-
ship ; but she was Marjorie in the flesh no
longer, and acted as the impartial agent of
Providence rather than as a party in the case,
being neither influenced by a sense of the
wrong she had suffered from him or the love

which she had cherished for him. When, therefore, the balladist imputes to her the language of judicial severity, he does so in strict accordance with her new character as defined by the mythology of the times; and, equally in accord with it, the sentence on the criminal was made heavy in order that he might have less expiation to suffer for it in the world to come.

> "Ye maunna Benjie head, brothers;
>   Ye maunna Benjie hang;
> But ye maun pyke out his twa grey e'en,
>   And punish him ere he gang.
>
> "Tie a green cravat round his neck,
>   And lead him out and in,
> And the best ac servant in the house
>   To wait young Benjie on.
>
> "And aye at every seven years' end,
>   Ye'll tak him to the linn;
> For that's the penance he maun dree
>   To scug his deadly sin."

YOUNG HUNTIN.

Another dreadful crime due to the promptings of "the green-eyed monster" is disclosed in our next tale. Young Huntin, its unfortu-

nate hero, acted contrary to the wise maxim,
" It's best to be off with the old love before ye
tak on with the new." While consorting with
Lady Maisry he had fallen under the bewitch-
ing spell of another damsel, and, manifesting
an amazing amount of effrontery, he called
upon his old sweetheart to bid her a final
adieu. She entreated him not to leave her—
to stay with her that night at all events, pro-
mising him abundance of good cheer, and
" charcoal clear, and candles burning bricht."
Declining her invitation with thanks, he told
her plump out the reason why—a maid by
Brannan's Well had now become the idol of
his heart. Disguising her feelings, Lady
Maisry renewed her solicitations, this time
with success—

> " O gin yer love be changed, my dear,
>   Since better canna be,
> At least ye will, for what has gane,
>   Bide this ae nicht wi me."

The faithless lover entered Maisry's bower
full of lusty life, but he never again saw the
light of day.

> When he was in her arms laid,
>   And gieing her kisses sweet,
> Then out she 's ta'en a little penknife,
>   And wounded him sae deep.

How to get rid of her victim, the gore-covered, ghastly evidence of her guilt?

> " O lang, lang is the winter nicht,
>   And slowly daws the day ;
> There is a dead man in my bower,
>   And I wish he were away."

> Up then spak her bower-maiden,
>   May Catherine was her name :
> " An there be a dead man in yer bower,
>   It 's yoursel' that has the blame."

Betray me not; render me help in my desperate straits; " heal this deed on me "; and the lady follows up this supplication to her maid with an appeal to her self-interest. Be my friend, good Catherine,

> " And the silks that were shapen for me sin'
>   Pasche,
> They shall be sewed for thee."

The services of the bower-maiden having been thus secured, the mistress and her accomplice resolved to pursue a scheme for making the death of young Huntin appear to be an accidental occurrence.

> They hae booted him and spurred him,
>   As he was wont to ride,

A hunting-horn around his neck,
　　A sharp sword by his side ;
And they hae sunk him, young Huntin,
　　In the deepest pot of Clyde.

But the murder would be out in spite of the ingenious scheme resorted to for hiding the evidence of it from the eye of man. Providence had its own witness in the form of a bonnie bird, which charged Lady Maisry with the crime. The little feathered accuser was asked by her to come down from his perch and sit upon her hand, and become her own darling pet. " No, no, no, the wee bird sang," I must keep out of your reach, else

　　" What ye hae done to young Huntin,
　　　　Sae wad ye do to me."

Huntin appears to have been a great favourite at Court. That very day he was expected to take part in a royal pageant, and the King, noticing his absence, sent a message of inquiry about him to Lady Maisry's bower. She, in reply, swore " by the green grass and the corn," that she had not seen the missing knight " sin' yesterday at morn ;" she adding, however,

　　" But ye 'll seek Clyde's water up and doun,
　　　　Ye 'll seek it out and in ;

> It fears me o' Clyde's water,
>   That he is drouned therein."

Every pool of the river was searched by divers, at the King's instance, without avail.

When justice seemed about to be baffled, the bonnie bird again appeared to play the *rôle* of an avenging Nemesis. He told the searchers to abandon their "douking in the day," and carry it on after dark, and then they would see candles burning bright over the pool where the dead man lay. Further, he impeached the two women with his murder, and told what he knew as to their disposal of his remains. The superstitious folk-lore of the period is strikingly illustrated in the verses that follow, describing the tests to which persons accused of murder were subjected in order to demonstrate their guilt or innocence.

> They left their douking in the day,
>   And douked in the nicht;
> And aboon the pot where Huntin lay
>   The candles they burned bricht.

> O white, white were his wounds washen,
>   As white as a linen clout;
> But when Lady Maisry she cam near,
>   The blude cam gushing oot.

As the wretched lady, in spite of this testimony, protested that her bower-woman must have perpetrated the deed, the King's judges resolved to test the truth of this charge by subjecting the accused to the ordeal of fire.

Then they hae made a big banefire,
　The bower-woman to brin ;
It wadna tak upon her cheek,
　Nor yet upon her chin,
But it took upon the cruel hands
　That put young Huntin in.

Then they 've ta'en out the bower-woman,
　And put the lady in ;
And first it took upon her cheek,
　And then upon her chin,
And syne it took on the fause, fause arms
　Young Huntin lay within.

SIR ROLAND.

The unfortunate hero of this ballad experienced similar treatment from his sweetheart, Lady Margaret, as that from which young Huntin suffered, only that in his case it seems to have been unprovoked. Sir Roland "tirl'd at his ain love's bower" late in the evening, and received from her a very effusive greeting—

> "O welcome, welcome, Sir Roland," she said,
>   " Thrice welcome thou art to me ;
> For this nicht thou will feast in my secret
>   bower,
>   And to-morrow we 'll wedded be."

Unprepared for such hasty nuptials, and warned by a night vision that the fair lady meant to play him false, he resolved to make his stay very short—

> " I dreamed a drearie dream yestreen,
>   And I wish it may come to gude ;
> I dreamed that ye slew my best grew-hound,
>   And gied me his lappered blude."

He urged also that the season was uncannie—

> " The nicht is Hallow-e'en," he said,
>   " 'The morn is Hallow-day,"

when the powers of darkness were abroad, and he must needs hasten homewards. But the treacherous siren would not be said nay —

> " Unbuckle your belt, Sir Roland," she said,
>   " And set you safely doun."

Overcome by her exuberant fondness, he at length complied with her request, though on being led into a gloomy apartment his suspicions were again aroused, and he obtruded the remark—

" O your chamber is very dark, fair maid,
    And the nicht is wondrous lown."

" Yes," she admitted—

" Dark, dark, is my secret bower,
And lonely it is at this midnicht hour ;
For there is none waking in a' this tower,
    But thou, my true love, and me."

Soon its waking occupiers were reduced to one, the lady owner of the mansion. How inexpressibly lonely it did seem now to her ; how dismally dark, too, even though the faint beams of a newly-risen moon were flickering in the chamber of death, making visible to her eyes the blood-covered corpse of her murdered lover. This lonely bower, with its new and terrible secret, was no place now for Lady Margaret, and, mounting on the dead man's steed, she rode away, heeding but little whither she went—

She hadna ridden a mile o' gate,
    Never a mile but ane,
When she was aware of a tall young man
    Slow riding owre the plain.

Like the mysterious mounted stranger who, late at night, thrust his company on Wandering Willie's gudesire, the " tall young man " kept persistently close to the fugitive damsel—

She turned her to the richt about,
  Then to the left turned she ;
But aye 'tween her and the wan munelicht,
  That tall knight did she see.

As if acting under a sudden impulse, she, giving up her attempt to ride out of his way, followed him fast and fell; but she failed to reach his side. Then opening up her mind to the mysterious horseman, the forlorn lady prayed him, if he were a leal true knight, to take pity upon her and win her love, for she " in dule was dight "—

But naething did the tall knight say,
  And naething did he blin ;
Still slowly rade he on before,
  And fast she rade behin'.

The black horse of her companion seemed to be only cantering, but her steed, though she whipped it and spurred it " till its breast was all a-foam," continued always in the rear. Again she cried in her anguish—

" O if you be a gay young knight,
  As well I trow you be,
Pull tight your bridle-reins, and stay
  Till I come up to thee."

But nothing did that tall knight say,
    And no whit did he blin,
Until he reached a broad river's side,
    And there he drew his rein.

Speaking for the first time—

" O is this water deep," he said,
    " As it is wondrous dun ?
Or is it sic as a saikless maid
    And a leal true knight may swim ?"

The lady having replied in the affirmative,
they entered the deep dark stream, " and
fast they baith swam doun."   Life was still
dear to Lady Margaret, though burdened by
her unspeakable crime.   How pitifully she,
who had been so pitiless to Sir Roland, en-
treated the unknown knight to save her from
becoming a prey to the merciless flood—

" The water weets my tae," she said,
    " The water weets my knee ;
Hold up my bridle-reins, sir knight,
    For the sake of our Ladie."

Probably our readers have already penetrated
through the disguise of the strange apparition.
His identity and purpose are revealed, in the
true ballad style, by the verses which follow—

" If I would help thee now," he said,
    " It were a deadly sin ;
For I 've sworn ne'er to trust a fair May's
        word,
    Till the water weets her chin."

" O the water weets my waist," she said,
    " Sae does it weet my chin,
And my aching heart rins round about.
    The burn maks sic a din.

" The water is waxing deeper still,
    Sae does it wax mair wide ;
And aye the further that we ride on,
    Farther off is the other side."

Little wotting the revelation that awaited her—
the falsest of womankind, she began to up-
braid him as " a false, false knight."   Turning
round in the middle of the river, he looked her
full in the face till " loudly she did scream."
The visage she confronted, wan, rueful, and
ghastly, was recognised by her as none other
than that of the handsome winsome knight
who had entered her bed-chamber in the flush
of manly strength a few hours ago.   Was this
the wraith of Sir Roland come to punish her
in the water for what she had done to him
in the bower ?   Very soon did he apprise the
miserable lady of his retributive mission, the

information being communicated in words of
scathing sarcasm—

> " O this is Hallow-morn," he said,
>   " And it is your bridal day ;
> But sad wad be that gay wedding,
>   If bridegroom and bride were away.

> " And ride on, ride on, proud Margaret,
>   Till the water comes owre your bree ;
> For the bride maun ride deep and deeper
>   yet,
>   Wha rides this ford wi' me.

> " Turn round, turn round, proud Margaret,
>   Turn ye round, and look on me ;
> Thou hast killed a true knight under trust,
>   And his ghost now links on wi' thee."

THE DEMON LOVER.

> " O where hae ye been, my lang-lost
>   love,
>   This lang seven years and more ? "
> " O I 'm come to seek my former vows
>   Ye granted me before."

The lady to whom these words were addressed
by an old sweetheart prayed him to be silent
about their past amours, and thus avoid bitter

strife. He had lost his chance, as she had given her hand to another.

> He turned him richt and round about,
>   And the tear blinded his e'e ;
> " I ne'er wad hae trodden on Irish ground,
>   If it hadna been for thee."

Following up his remonstrance, he affirmed that but for his love for her he might have received a king's daughter in marriage. " Blame yourself for losing such a match," retorted the saucy madam in effect ; but, deeply troubled by his distress, she began to pity him with " the pity that is akin to love." When in this perilous mood, the thought entered her mind—Ought I not to fulfil my virgin vows, even at the expense of those made by me at the altar ? Acting, as it soon appeared, under unearthly, malignant influences, which gave irresistible force to her lover's plea, she became his willing victim. A precautionary inquiry from her brought a captivating response from him, which sealed her doom—

> " If I was to leave my husband dear,
>   And my twa babes also,
> O where is it you wad tak me to,
>   If I with thee should go ? "

> " I hae seven ships upon the sea,
>   The eighth brought me to land,

With four-and-twenty bold mariners,
  And music on ilka hand."

She has taken up her twa little babes,
  Kissed them baith cheek and chin :
" O fare ye weel, my ain twa babes,
  For I 'll never see you again."

She set her foot upon the ship—
  No mariners could she behold ;
But the sails were o' the taffetie,
  And the masts o' the beaten gold.

On the wide world of waters, not a soul beside
her except the mysterious being for whose
sake she had left home, husband, children,
surrendered her purity, and bartered away her
mental peace. A terrible host of sacrifices
truly. Yes; but he will compensate for the
loss with the inexhaustible treasures of his
love, and we shall be all in all to each other.
If ever the poor fugitive matron sought con-
solation in such anticipations, their utter
falsity would soon have become apparent.

They hadna sailed a league, a league,
  A league, but barely three,
When dismal grew his countenance,
  And drumlie grew his e'e.

The masts that were like the beaten
          gold,
    Bent not on the heaving seas ;
The sails that were o' the taffetie,
    Filled not in the east land breeze.

They hadna sailed a league, a league,
    A league, but barely three,
Until she espied his cloven hoof,
    And she wept richt bitterlie.

The balladist does not tell us how far the
human nature of the lady's lover had been
overborne by the fiendish nature that was
symbolised by his cloven foot. Such moot
points in the popular mythology of the period
lay beyond the minstrel's ken. It was his
business to sing of these mysteries, not to
analyse or scrutinise them closely. Besides,
any revelation that would have rendered them
more intelligible and less unfamiliar might
have interfered with that sense of wonder to
which ballads of this mystical class appeal.
And marvel is heaped upon marvel in the
verses that remain of "The Demon Lover."

    " O haud your tongue, of your weeping,"
          he says,
    " Of your weeping now let me be ;
I will show you how the lilies grow
    On the banks of Italy."

" O what hills are yon, yon pleasant hills,
    That the sun shines sweetly on ?"
" O yon are hills of heaven," he said,
    Where you will never win."

" O what'n a mountain 's yon," she said,
    " Sae dreary wi' frost and snow ?"
" O yon is the mountain of hell," he cried,
    " Where you and I maun go !"

And aye when she turned her round
        aboot,
    Aye taller he seemed for to be ;
Until that the taps of that gallant ship
    Nae taller were than he.

The presentiment of the guilty wife and
mother that, when taking leave of her two
babes, she would never see them again, proved
only too true. Putting forth his last destruc-
tive effort, the man-fiend

Struck the tap-mast wi' his hand,
    The fore-mast wi' his knee ;
And he brak that gallant ship in twain,
    And sunk her in the sea.

THE ELFIN KNIGHT.

Captivated by a knight of Elf-land, as Janet was with Tamlane, the heroine of this old lay was sadly put about when, on offering him her hand, he declined it, alleging that she was too young for wedded life. " I hae a sister younger than me," said the amorous maiden. " and she was married yesterday." But the gentleman-fairy, though not averse to a little game of flirtation, knew full well that wedlock in this case would answer badly for both bride and bridegroom, and he prescribed to the lady a series of impracticable tasks, telling her that when she performed them, but not till then, he would make her his wife. Here is what he said, either in mockery of her suit, or as a colourable pretext for getting rid of it and her—

> " Married to me ye shall be nane
>   (Blaw, blaw, blaw winds, blaw),
> Till ye mak me a sark without a seam
>   (And the wind has blawn my plaid awa)."

Not only was she to make the shirt seamless, but, according to further instructions, she was to " shape it knifeless, shearless," and " sew it needle - threadless," the directions closing thus—

" And ye maun wash it within a well
    (Blaw, blaw, blaw winds, blaw),
Where dew never wat, nor rain ever fell
    (And the wind has blawn my plaid
        awa).

" And ye maun dry it upon a thorn
    (Blaw, blaw, blaw winds, blaw),
That never budded sin Adam was born
    (And the wind has blawn my plaid
        awa)."

By this time the lady was beginning to see
that she had made a mistake in fixing her
affections on a mongrel being, who was neither
lovingly human nor yet half so divine as he
appeared to be at their first interview. The
balladist goes on to tell how cleverly she
foiled the cold-blooded, tantalising knight
with his own weapons.

" O gin that kindness I do for thee,
    There's something ye maun do for me."

That something bearing on the culture of a
piece of ground (her marriage portion, I sup-
pose), which he was asked to undertake with
tiny implements and offices that were propor-
tioned to his dimensions as a fairy mannikin.
Both satire and humour abound in the con-
ditions which she lays down.

> " I hae an acre o' gude lea-land
>   (Blaw, blaw, blaw winds, blaw),
> Between the saut sea and the strand
>   (And the wind has blawn my plaid
>   awa). "

The recurring over-words need not be re-peated in the further instructions which she gives.

> " Ye 'll plough it wi' your blawing-horn,
> And ye will sow it wi' pepper corn.

> " And ye maun harrow 't wi' a single tyne,
> And shear it wi' a sheep's shank-bane.

> " And big a cairt o' lime and stane,
> And Robin Redbreist maun trail it hame.

> " And ye maun barn it in a mouse-hole,
> And ye maun thrash it in your shoe-sole.

> " And ye maun winnow it in your loof,
> And ye maun sack it in your glove.

> " And ye maun dry it but candle or coal,
> And ye maun grind it but quern or mill.

When these feats are performed, said the nymph, with a flourish—

> " When ye hae done and finished your wark,
> Then come to me and ye'se get your sark ! "

But the elfin knight, finding that she was disenchanted, and that in her he had met with more than his match, declined to clench the bargain. When the curtain falls, the lady is left cured of her love-fit, " in maiden meditation, fancy free."

THE CRUEL MOTHER.

" Ah, well-a-day! the wind gies by, and will not stay." Not even when an unmarried mother leaves home by stealth, gives birth to two babies, binds them hand and feet, stabs them to the heart, and buries them secretly out of sight. The insensate wind sweeps past, quite as unaffected by the tragical events as if it had not blown fiercely on the blood-stained hands of the infanticide, and played caressingly with the silken hair of her innocent victims. No earthly agency proclaims her guilt, and had not witnesses to it come from on high, she might have passed through life as a " maiden leal," or gone to the matrimonial altar as a virtuous bride. The cruel mother returns to her father's halls, carrying her head high, playing the part all through of a pure, sweet, tender-hearted damsel; which conduct draws forth from the narrator of the tale his old lament, " Ah, well-a-day! the wind gies by, and will not stay" to blow away the hypocritical mask that hides her fearful secret. As she is standing at her bower-door, however, on a certain day, two lovely little creatures flee through the firmament, and appear before her bewildered gaze. Addressing them, she said—

> " Look not sae, bonnie babies ;
>   Gin ye smile sae, ye 'll smile me dead."

> " O, bonnie babes, gin ye were mine,
>   I would dress you up in satins fine ;
> O I would dress you in the silk,
>   And wash you aye in the morning milk."

Their response is judicially severe—it can scarcely be called unduly merciless. It is effectively rounded off by the minstrel's old refrain—

> " O wild mother, when we were thine ;
>   Ah, well-a-day !
> You clothed us not in silk sae fine ;
>   The wind gies by, and will not stay.

> " O cruel mother, we were thine ;
>   Ah, well-a-day !
> And then you made us wear the twine ;
>   The wind gies by, and will not stay.

" But now we 're in the heavens high ;
  Ah, well-a-day !
And you 've the pains of hell to try ;
  The wind gies by, and will not stay."

THE WIFE OF USHER'S WELL.

I close our intercourse with the old minstrels by giving one of their most charming effusions, the tenor of which presents a striking contrast to that of the preceding tale, showing as it does how maternal love prevailed with Heaven to send from Hades three young men to comfort their despairing mother. A wealthy wife, we are told, once lived at Usher's Well who had three stalwart sons, all of whom went to sea. Like the children of the Patriarch, they were all cut off in one day—after a bare week's absence, they were drowned in the deep ; and the news of their sad fate so overwhelmed the matron that she refused to be comforted, and in the depths of her desolation prayed—

" I wish the wind may never cease,
  Nor freshes in the flood,
Till my three sons come hame to me,
  In earthly flesh and blood."

A terrible imprecation ! She had lost her earthly all, and desired that storms might rage perpetually in sea and river, so that others might suffer as well as she, unless her sons were returned to her, full of lusty life, as when, three short weeks ago, she last beheld them— a wish she could scarcely hope to be realised. Strange to say, they came, not as mere wraiths, but body and spirit conjoined — their very selves—the bodies from the bottom of the deep, or grave dug by the lone sea-shore, their spirits from within the gates of the glorified city above—all this being quite in accordance with a belief current in the minstrel age, and not yet altogether exploded. In keeping with the rabbinical idea, the young men wore garlands—the most distinctive part being their head-gear, a chaplet woven from the boughs of the sacred birch. It is only by an inference to be drawn from their dress, and from the place where it grew, that we know they are visitors from the world unseen ; but this indirect mode of description is often used, as we have seen, with the best effect by the ballad-artists. The mystical portion of the ballad under notice is introduced in a style of simple gloom and grandeur which nothing can surpass :

It fell about the Martinmas,
  When nichts are lang and mirk,
The carline wife's three sons cam hame,
  And their hats were o' the birk.

It neither grew in syke nor ditch,
  Nor yet in ony sheugh,
But at the gates of Paradise
  That birk grew fair eneugh.

What raptures filled the mother's heart when she once more clasped her lost boys to her bosom! A feast is prepared; then she has them laid in bed, and, lest her precious ones be again stolen from her sight, she sits down a watcher by the bed-side; but, overcome by exhaustion, she slumbers, and the three youths glide reluctantly away on a summons which they have no power to resist. No remarks of mine, however, are called for to elucidate the touching traits of this primitive ballad, whose atmosphere is of that mystic border country which partakes of both earth and heaven, where the gushings and strivings of strong human love overleap the boundary of the spirit land. "Blow up the fire," says the exulting matron—

"Blow up the fire now, maidens mine,
  Bring water from the well,
For a' my house shall feast this nicht,
  Since my three sons are well."

And she has made to them a bed,
  She 's made it large and wide,
And she 's ta'en her mantle her about,
  Sat down at the bed-side.

Up then crew the red, red cock,
  And up and crew the gray ;
The eldest to the youngest said :
  " 'Tis time we were away.

" The cock doth craw, the day doth daw,
  The channerin worm doth chide ;
Gin we be missed out o' our place,
  A sair pain we maun bide."

But the youngest—probably the favourite son
—would fain stay a little longer with his
mother, and pictures her distress when she
finds them gone :

" Lie still, lie still, but a little wee while,
  Lie still but if we may ;
Gin my mother should miss us when she
      wakes,
  She 'll gae mad ere it be day."

O it 's they 've ta'en up their mother's
      mantle,
  And they 've hung it on a pin :
" O lang may ye hing, my mother's mantle,
  Ere ye hap us again."

" Fare ye weel, my mother dear,
    Fareweel to barn and byre,
And fare ye weel, the bonnie lass
    That kindles my mother's fire."

FINIS.

Printed by T. and A. CONSTABLE, Printers to Her Majesty,
at the Edinburgh University Press.